God and Man in Time

A CHRISTIAN APPROACH TO HISTORIOGRAPHY

Earle E. Cairns

BAKER BOOK HOUSE
Grand Rapids, Michigan

ISBN: 0-8010-2426-9

Library of Congress
Catalog Card Number: 78-73042

All Scripture quotations are, unless otherwise noted, from the Authorized (King James) Version.

PHOTOLITHOPRINTED BY CUSHING - MALLOY, INC.
ANN ARBOR, MICHIGAN, UNITED STATES OF AMERICA
1979

***TO
JOANN***

Contents

Preface

Until the twentieth century man was optimistic about his future. During the Renaissance, the eighteenth-century Enlightenment, and the optimistic nineteenth century, man thought himself to be born good and perfectible rather than sinful and an heir to original depravity. Man with his rational powers, using the scientific method as a tool, could create Utopia on earth with or without God. The beckoning goal of a perfect world order seemed within reach. Material progress through applied science was mistaken for political order and spiritual progress.

The dream of progress to perfection faded with international depression in 1929 and two world wars, and men have become increasingly pessimistic about any future "brave new world." The enlargement of the borders of science has seemed to push God into a corner or even out of the universe. This leaves man feeling alone in a universe that often seems hostile to him with its frequent vast and impersonal disasters—uncontrollable floods, hurricanes, earthquakes. Man seems so weak, finite, inadequate, and alone in impersonal nature. In addition he seems bent on ignorantly polluting his environment to the point of its becoming a threat to his survival.

Political crisis can be added to the cosmic crisis. The nineteenth-century dream that economic interdependence would lead to political unification has been destroyed by racial nationalism (as in Germany), two brutal world wars, worldwide depression, and the possibility of another apocalyptic world war marked by atomic, bacteriological, and chemical warfare. Genocide has become a possibility. Famine and starvation threaten a large part of the world's population. Collectivism in economic and political life has followed the collapse of rising expectations. Demonic forces seem to be loosed in human history.

Modern man also faces a personal crisis. He has lost confidence in his ability to deal with crises in history and can find no answers for his problems within himself or his culture. The dream of indefinite progress to Utopia through science has faded in the face of universal depravity, and many have been gripped by existential despair. The cosmic, social, and personal crises seem to have moral and spiritual roots. Can the careful study of man's past help him face these crises?

Many, especially young people, think history has no meaning because the past has no relevance for them. They agree with Henry Ford's dictum that history is "bunk," or with Voltaire's declaration that history is "little more than the history of crime" or "a pack of tricks that we play on the dead." Others agree with Georg Hegel's comment that the only thing history teaches is that people and governments have never learned anything from history. Unfortunately such people only prove the truth of George Santayana's belief that those who forget history are bound to repeat it, making the same mistakes others have in the past. Cicero is credited with the idea that those who do not know what took place before they were born will remain children forever.

History does have something to offer to man in his search for meaning in life, in spite of these pessimistic or cynical views of history. Paul in his letters to the Corinthians and Romans told them that biblical history would reveal which courses to avoid and which to follow. Ancient and medieval historians believed that history has a didactic or teaching function and will impart wisdom and inculcate morality. The author agrees that history has a worthwhile function in the present.

Part of the blame for history's lack of appeal belongs to professional historians who have written technical, often dry and dull monographs for their fellow historians. Others, with John B. Bury, preoccupied with the existential, laud history as "a science, no less and no more," that is to be studied merely for its own sake. Henry Brooks Adams and others have been enamored with the idea that by applying the scientific method to the data of history, they might find social laws in history that are as valid as laws of science. Others have adopted such a relativistic outlook that history becomes merely "contemporary thought about the past," which precludes any worthwhile reconstruction of past events. The scientific approach leads to pride, the relativistic approach to historical skepticism. Either the truth lies between these extremes or the nearly twenty thousand historians in the American Historical Association are wasting their time studying, teaching, and writing history. We need not be skeptical about the objectivity of historical facts that can be discovered by the scientific method, even though we recognize elements of subjectivity in their interpretation.

Scientific analysis of historical records will never produce universal laws like those in the more exact natural sciences. But the historian can study historical sources by scientific methods and make valid inductions from his facts about incidents in the past, inductions that will gain a consensus among historians. He can also develop general causation that makes clear the contingent causative role in history of such secondary factors as the geographic, economic, religious, and intellectual. He will also, implicitly if not explicitly, finally relate his materials to some ultimate frame of reference that will unify the parts into a meaningful whole and relate them to reality. Any historical interpretation must cope with the issues of man's origin, actions in time and space, and final destiny. Man's failure in history and the frustration or defeat of his high hopes cannot be ignored. If shut out of the front door, philosophy will creep in the back door.

Luke presented an excellent summary of the process of historical study in the prologue of his Gospel (1:1–4). He viewed it as scientific in method, philosophic in interpretation, and artistic in presentation. He sought out firsthand as well as secondary records, studied them with scientific methodology, and related his findings to his goal of determining the truth concerning Christ.

The author will follow Luke's pattern[1] by discussing the scientific, philosophic, and artistic aspects of the historian's reconstruction of the past, in that order. Consideration of how history is written may well make history more interesting to those who read it and more relevant to our day. The writer is deeply conscious of and grateful to the generations of students who in his classes on historical methods for over twenty-five years have tested his theories with sound questions and helped him refine his ideas.

The personal names in this book have, where possible, been conformed to the style of the 1976 edition of *Webster's Biographical Dictionary.*

1. This pattern is also suggested in Louis R. Gottschalk, *Understanding History: A Primer of Historical Method,* p. viii; Allan Nevins, *The Gateway to History,* pp. 44–45; and especially George M. Trevelyan, *"Clio, a Muse" and Other Essays Literary and Pedestrian,* new ed. (New York: Longmans and Green, 1930), pp. 142–43, 169.

Introduction: The Nature of History

Consideration of the nature of history at once raises the question of how to define it. Is it merely the events of the past, the record of those events, the research into those records for information about the past, the interpretive reconstruction of the past, or the artistic restatement of the author's understanding of the past?

Definitions

Historiography is a term commonly used by historians. The reader with some linguistic background will recognize that it comes from two Greek words that mean the writing (*graphē*) of history (*historia*). The term *historiography* is sometimes used to mean the process of writing history, which includes the gathering of documents; critical research to validate each document's authenticity, genuineness, and integrity; the interpretation of the data; and the imaginative written restatement of past events. Thus conceived, historiography is the discipline of historical writing. More often historians follow the lead of Carl L. Becker in defining *historiography* as "the study of the history of historical study."[1] The author agrees with Becker even though the first definition well defines the process of historical study and writing.

The accompanying chart shows that the definition of *history* is more complicated; it is used in more ways, and each meaning has some validity. *History* may be defined first as an **incident** or actual event in time and space. This is history as actuality or reality. This idea has been expressed by German historians as *geschichte,* derived from the verb *geschehen,* "to happen." History in this sense is "a happening" in the past. This event is absolute and objective. It can be known by God alone because for Him there is no time in the sense there is for man. Man can only know directly the existential historical event in which he participates.

History thus conceived can never be repeated. One cannot dogmatize that history repeats itself. There can be parallel or similar actions in different time-and-space settings because man is man and may act similarly under similar circumstances. But Plato will never be repeated in later history, though there may be philosophers who also philosophize in their day as Plato did in his. History as incident or event is thus a primary definition of the word.

The historian usually does not work directly on the events of the past. With the exception of the materials provided by archaeology, which give direct information about the past, he must rely upon indirect records of the past. This indirect **information,** known as records, relics, remains, or recollections by contemporaries or later persons of past events, constitutes a second way to define *history.* The historian has to study indirect presentations of the past rather than the past directly. In this manner he is more limited than the scientist, who studies his data directly and objectively in the present.

These remains may be fossils or artifacts, objects made by man for his everyday use, not for the information of future historians. King Tutankhamen's heavy gold casket, one of several in which he was buried, is an example of a direct record of the past. Records are more often documents written on stone, leather, brick, papyrus, or paper that

1. "What Is Historiography?" *The American Historical Review* 44 (1938): 20.

CHART 1

← Geschichte →	← Historia	→		← Historikos →	
		← Scientific	→	← Philosophic →	← Artistic →
Incident	Information	Inquiry	Induction	Interpretation	Impartation
Result of human action in time and space	Records, Relics, and Remains	Research		Reconstruction	
	← Analysis		→	← Synthesis →	
History as event or "happening"; actuality. The "stuff" of history.	History as: 1. Records (written or oral) 2. Relics 3. Remains	History as discipline or process	History as logic	History as thought or product	History as art or literature (exposition)
Exists objectively to historian, but is fully known only to God. Is unrepeatable, occurring only once in time and space; parallels and patterns can be seen.	Records consist of: 1. Fossils 2. Artifacts 3. Documents Remains often marred by: 1. Incompleteness 2. Indirectness 3. Involvement of recorder or historian 4. Invention	Steps of process: 1. Collect documents 2. Criticize documents 3. Classify data		Schools: 1. Geographic 2. Economic 3. Biographic Philosophies: 1. Pessimistic 2. Optimistic 3. Pessimistic-optimistic	
	Gives a record or knowledge of reality.	Gives facts about reality.		Gives ultimate meaning of facts.	
Facts	Facts accumulated (facts objective to the historian)	Facts established	Facts organized	Facts interpreted	Facts presented (with maximum correspondence to reality)
	Luke 1:1–2; Gal. 1:1–2	Luke 1:3	← Luke 1:4	→	Luke 1:3
	← Accumulate, establish facts (Who? What? When? Where?)		→	Interpret facts (Why?)	Present facts (How?)
	← Knowledge	→	← Understanding →	← Wisdom →	
← Absolute, objective →	← Relative, somewhat subjective				→

transmit information about the past. Primary or original sources, which are contemporary with the incident described, are what interest the historian most.

Herodotus used the word *historia* in the sense of inquiry into or investigation of the records, sites, and remains of the past. Our word *history* is derived through the Latin from the word he used. Paul used an aorist form of this word in Galatians 1:18, *historēsai,* which is translated "see" in the King James Version. Paul used it in the sense of "investigate." Paul went up to Jerusalem to investigate, to get from Peter firsthand information about Christ. This constitutes history as record or information.

A third meaning of history is that of **inquiry** or research. History in this sense is the discipline governing research into the past. After gathering his data, the historian uses a technique or discipline that enables him critically to test the records of the past for authenticity, genuineness, and integrity. Herodotus critically interviewed witnesses, studied records, visited sites of historic events, and drew upon his own recollections in writing his account of the war between the Persians and the Greeks. History in the sense of inquiry or research may be described as the discipline or process of discovering, collecting, and testing data about the past.

A fourth definition of history is the subjective **interpretation,** reconstruction, or restatement of past space-time events. Homer's *Illiad* was thought of as *historikos,* the final record by the narrator of the actual event. No reconstruction of an event can ever be perfect, but as historians verify one another's work, a consensus can emerge to give men a fairly accurate understanding of the event.

One must not forget that the historian always tends in some respects to reflect the opinions of his times or his own outlook on life. Personal and contemporary views constitute, in Becker's words, the writer's "climate of opinion." In the transition from event to final written record of the event, this climate of opinion is an important factor.

Some may feel that history is the imaginative **impartation** of the results of research and interpretation in written or oral form. This is the artistic or literary side of history that some historians have neglected in their preoccupation with the opinion of their fellow historians. Sir Winston Churchill and others have given attention to this side of history and have consequently enjoyed a wide readership.

History can thus be conceived in terms of human *incidents* in time and space that are socially significant to man, *information* (or records of those events), *inquiry* (or critical research of the records), *inductions* from the data, the historian's *interpretation* of the data, and the literary or oral *impartation* of the interpreted data. Most students study history in the last two senses.

History, as man can know it only after the once-for-all event in time and space, may be defined as *the interpreted literary reconstruction of the socially significant human past, based on data from documents studied by scientific methods.* The word *interpreted* is used because written history will always to some extent reflect the outlook of the age or the author. It can be scientific in the method used to study critically the records. The study may be in narrative, biographic, monographic, or textual form.

The historian's goal in all his work is truth concerning the past, just as Luke's goal in his biography of Christ was the truth concerning the life of Christ. Truth in the absolute sense will elude the historian, but he will give as true and complete an account of events as his records and frame of reference permit.

Both the Christian historian and his secular counterpart will use the same information about the past and after careful inquiry will develop inductions from their data. But when it comes to interpreting those inductions, each will fit them into a different ultimate frame of reference. Both will seek to impart their findings artistically so as to interest the reader.

History and Science

Can the historian, like the chemist, speak of his work as an exact science, or must he say that while he uses the scientific method, he will never achieve the same results as in the exact sciences? During the last half of the nineteenth century, historians increasingly thought of history as a science in both methods and results. They believed, with the great German historian Leopold von Ranke, that the historian could write "*geschichte wie es eigentlich gewesen*" (history as it actually happened). Von Ranke's insistence that one can exactly reconstruct the past from existing records was what led the American Historical Association, shortly after its inception in 1884, to make him its first honorary member. Increasingly between 1890 and 1930 in Europe and since 1930 in America, historians have challenged this concept. They hold that a past event can never be exactly reconstructed; many of them consider history to be simply "contemporary thought upon the past."

This issue raises philosophical questions in two areas. Critical philosophy, or epistemology, deals with how we can know reality and is concerned with the analytical aspect of history. Speculative philosophy, or ontology or metaphysics, deals with the nature of ultimate reality and is concerned with the synthetic dimension of history, with the relating of the historical parts to the whole. The first is more concerned with the method of history; the second, with relating the historian's findings, meaningfully synthesized, to reality, linking the here and now with the then and with eternity. The first involves the scientific aspect of history; the second an ultimate, and in the case of the Christian historian, the revelational aspect of history. Both are from God, the first involving the how of historical study and the second the why of history or the philosophy of history.

While historians have divided into many schools and while some have not been true to their main implicit premises, two major conflicting outlooks have developed in this century concerning historical epistemology. The first emphasizes the objective side of history, the second the subjective. Leopold von Ranke (1795–1886) is the patron saint of the first school because of his claim that the historian can exactly reconstruct the past. His disciples forget that even he found covering laws of providence in the historical process. They believe that written history is an exact scientific reconstruction of the past. Historians of the second school think of history as something the historian writes as he relives or thinks about the past.

Scientific, positivistic, academic, objectivist, and *historicist* are terms that have been used to describe those who think history can be as exact as science in its method. Such historians seek to "tell it like it was." John B. Bury (1861–1927), in his inaugural lecture in January 1903 as regius professor of history at Cambridge University, said it is not "superfluous" to insist that history is "a science, no less and no more." The French historian Fustel de Coulanges in 1862 is said to have told his students not to applaud him when he lectured well; it is "not I who speak but history which speaks through me." History to him "is and should be a science." Karl Marx and Auguste Comte also believed they wrote scientific history. Carroll Quigley, a more recent historian, considered his work to be the result of scientific study.[2]

Other scientific historians thought that the study of history might even yield valid universal laws that would explain history to those who studied and read it. Henry T. Buckle (1821–1862), writing in 1857, thought that scientific, inductive historical study would let the historian see causal uniformities or laws of social development.[3] Study of food, soil, climate, and geography, as well as of economics, would lead to the discovery of principles according to which civilizations develop and decline. Henry Brooks Adams (1838–1918) was disappointed when he did not find the universal laws he sought by his scientific study of the records of the past. Comte (1798–1857) was sure that historical study would yield laws that could be used for social engineering and that would be as universal as those in science. E. P. Cheyney (1861–1947), in his presidential address to the American Historical Association in December 1923, spoke of laws of continuity, democracy, mutability, interdependence, free consent, and moral progress that he believed he had found through historical study.[4] Karl Popper and more recently Carl G. Hempel both contended for the possibility of professional historians, in the course of their study, discerning some covering, scientifically based laws.

There is much to commend in this view of history as science. A hard core of facts does exist independently of the historian and his interpretation, and upon these there is consensus among historians. Nikolai Lenin's return to Russia from Switzerland in a sealed railway car by permission of the Germans is a fact of history universally established and accepted. The divorce of Henry VIII from Catherine is another fact of history, one that was related to the coming of the Reformation in England. The writing and publication of *Uncle Tom's Cabin* is a historical fact, but the extent of its influence is a matter of interpretation. The historian in determining these facts will be as impartial and honest as the scien-

2. *The Evolution of Civilizations: An Introduction to Historical Analysis* (New York: Macmillan, 1961).

3. *History of Civilization in England*, 2 vols. (London: Parker, 1857–1861).

4. "Law in History," *The American Historical Review* 29 (1924): 231–48.

tist in his laboratory, even if he does sometimes find himself a part of his data. The historian can even make valid inductions from his scientifically derived data, but when he seeks to integrate his data into an ultimate, meaningful synthesis, he will be influenced by the intellectual climate in which he works or by his own experience. The development of universally valid scientific laws in history cannot be realized even though historical records are studied by scientific methods.

Most of those writing on the epistemology of history have been philosophers who have had little or no experience in the scientific study and writing of history. This has led them to throw out the baby with the bath. Some have become agnostic about the possibility of reconstructing past events. They insist that because records have been filtered through human minds, historical facts have no existence apart from the thinker, and the historian today simply thinks about the past.

Those who oppose the scientific study of history are known as romanticists, idealists, relativists, or subjectivists. Seemingly influenced by German idealism, this group of historians emerged in Germany and England in opposition to scientific historians, but it has won many disciples in the United States since 1930. Most of them are philosophers rather than practicing historians.

Wilhelm Dilthey (1833–1911), the son of a Protestant minister in the Rhineland, was professor of philosophy for over thirty years in the Universities of Breslau and Berlin. Though scientific historical study could give historical facts, he believed subjectivity would characterize the selection of areas to study as well as the interpretation of facts. More important, he believed that history could be little more than the historian's "reliving of the past."

Robin G. Collingwood (1889–1943), a teacher for many years at Oxford, took the position in *The Idea of History* that history is really abstract and subjective thought about the past, even though it is based to some extent on scientifically garnered evidence.[5] Historical truth is individual rather than universal because it is the reenactment in the historian's mind of the past. The Italian philosopher and historian Benedetto Croce (1866–1952) described history as "contemporary

5. *The Idea of History* (Oxford: Clarendon, 1946).

thought upon the past." These men all thought of written history as subjective and relative rather than objective.

Carl L. Becker (1873–1945) and Charles A. Beard (1874–1948) adapted these ideas to the American historical scene in their reaction against the scientific school during the post–World War I era. In his address "What Are Historical Facts?" given to the American Historical Association in December 1926, and in his essay "Everyman His Own Historian" (1932),[6] Becker emphasized the historian's selection of topics and facts to study; the filtering of historical facts through the minds of the recorders; the symbolic nature of words, which tell of events whose origin is outside the historian's present experience; and the fact that the historian can do little more than reflect on these ideas, which are largely the creation of his own mind. In his essay "Written History as an Act of Faith" (1934), Beard also subscribed to relativism in historical study. The selection of a topic cuts it off from the universal, and in his selection and interpretation of facts, the historian is conditioned by his personal and temporal environment.[7] The publication in 1946 by the Social Science Research Council of *Theory and Practice in Historical Study: A Report of the Committee on Historiography* (SSRC bulletin no. 54) provided an expression of the relativistic position that influenced a whole generation of American historians. More recent existentialist philosophy as well as past German idealism has strengthened the hold of relativistic historical interpretation on the historical profession in the United States. This conception of history may well lead ultimately to historical skepticism, according to which history can be only an intellectual exercise, the historian's reflecting on the past. This school of history did, however, call attention to the human element in historical study—the historian himself, his temporal and personal biases.

Elements of truth in both of these opposing groups can be useful in historical thought and writing. The scientific historians and even many of the relativists believe that while historical evidence is usually indirect, incomplete, invented by man, and subject to the historian's selection, the historian can, as his work is objectively verified and checked by other

6. "Everyman His Own Historian," *The American Historical Review* 37 (1932): 221–36.

7. "Written History as an Act of Faith," *The American Historical Review* 39 (1934): 219–31.

historians, discover facts about the past from which valid inductions can be made. The relativistic historians on the other hand are correct in their claim that the historian's personal outlook and the life view of his age will influence his interpretation. Reconstruction of the past will never exactly correspond with the events of the past.

The conflicting claims of these two groups revolve around the question of how far history can be scientific. Science may be described as systematized, objective general truths and laws about a subject that are established by scientific methodology. The selection of a problem, tentative hypothesis, experiment and observation, verification through repeated experiments by the scientist and his colleagues, and the formulation of a general or covering law enter into a scientific method. Even though the historian cannot usually have direct contact with his data—the exception is the field of archaeology—it should be noted that scientists such as astronomers and geologists cannot always have direct contact either. Relativistic historians complain that historical data is indirect, often incomplete, and suffers from interpretation that grows out of environmental and personal biases.

Marked differences between history and science will keep history from being an exact science. Such differences are developed in chart 2. These points of difference reveal that history may be scientific in method but can never be as exact as such sciences as chemistry and physics.

Both history and even exact science have limitations. Both are finite because God has not revealed everything to man (Deut. 29:29; Ps. 115:16; I Peter 1:10–12; cf. Gen. 1:26, 28; 3:5–6, 22). The truth man knows is partial and incomplete (I Cor. 13:9–12), and man is transitory (Pss. 144:4; 146:3–4). Man's free will makes for uniqueness in history, and all his work is marred by his having fallen in Adam and by his sinfulness (Rom. 1:19–32; 5:12, 19). Fallibility because of these things is a characteristic of man's best work.

This all demonstrates that history cannot be as exact a science as chemistry is, but that the historian can use scientific methodology in getting facts from records. He will avoid the Scylla of history as a mere compilation of data in the name of science and the Charybdis of history as only the subjective product of historical thought. The relativists rightly point out the indirectness, incompleteness, and inadequacy

CHART 2

HISTORY	SCIENCE
Is a study of something dynamic—a process affected by man's free will.	Is a study of something static and uniform—the things of nature.
Depends on indirect testimony and data.	Depends on fixed data.
Is a study of unique, unrepeatable events.	Is a study of repeatable, recurrent data.
Yields possible generalizations and patterns.	Yields laws of general application.
Involves the historian—his personal and environmental biases.	Does not involve the scientist; he is not part of his data.
Has flexible vocabulary.	Has fixed vocabulary.
Does not predict.	Predicts and controls.
Describes reality.	Observes real things directly.
Allows no repetition or control of data.	Allows control of experiments.

of data in many cases, and the personal and environmental influences on the one doing the interpreting. They forget, however, that there is a hard core of facts about events which can be verified by the critical scrutiny of historians, so that a consensus can be reached about most historical information. They also forget that valid inductions can be derived from the data apart from the philosophical and psychological outlook of the researcher. The author's study of missionaries in Africa led to inductions concerning their work in education, road-building, introduction of new crops, and exploration.

But when one asks the meaning of his data, the historian is conditioned by personal and temporal factors. Neither von Ranke's ideal of reconstructing history exactly nor Dilthey's relativism is adequate. Historical study can yield accurate knowledge to the extent that the historian is honest, impartial, and neutral in discovering data. He knows he can never create universal laws as valid as those of more-exact sciences to help control or accurately predict the future, but the Christian historian can join in "understanding and knowing temporal reality scientifically."

History and Social Science

Organized study of social science dates only from the middle of the eighteenth century. It grew out of the optimistic idea that perfectible man, by using the scientific method and reason, can conquer nature and in time produce a perfect social environment. Social science would do for men what science can do in controlling nature for human use and welfare. By rational use of the scientific method in human affairs, historians could ascertain social laws as valid as laws in the physical sciences. These social laws could be used to predict and control human development and institutions. Such was the outlook of Marx and Comte in the nineteenth century. Because man is perfectible and a sinner only by choice rather than by heredity, they believed, man can achieve perfection in time.

Most definitions of social science lack any Christian orientation and rest on an optimistic view of human nature. Both behavioral and social science are characterized by dependence on the scientific method. Behavioral studies such as psychology focus more on individual or small-group behavior than on collective behavior. They also lay more stress on empirical methods, the possibility of deriving "laws" from empirical study and of using these to predict and control social and individual behavior. Thus many psychologists use laboratory work to study behavior, political scientists use the computer to study voting patterns, and the economist employs the computer to analyze economic patterns with a view to controlling the business cycle.

The social scientist concentrates more on the study of group or collective behavior but is more modest than the behaviorally oriented social scientist when it comes to finding "laws" in his data and attempting to predict and control human actions. Social science may be defined as the study of man in society or in groups, using scientific methods to discover underlying uniformities that may be useful to society. Most social and behavioral scientists assume human nature to be not fallible but perfectible; the scholar with a Christian orientation of course recognizes God's creatorship and man's fallenness.

Several disciplines are linked with the social and behavioral sciences. History is the oldest of the social sciences, whether considered as record or reconstruction, although the data of the other social sciences has also been present since the creation of man. Political science began with the deductive studies of Plato and the inductive studies of Aristotle concerning the origin and nature of the state. Economics, although not known by that name, was studied by the ancients. Geography, sociology, anthropology, and the youngest social science, psychology, have been developed as disciplines since about 1750. Division of function and specialization have helped to make them separate disciplines. These social sciences are distinct from the humanities, such as the fine arts, literature, and philosophy, and from the natural sciences, such as biology, chemistry, and physics. Some class the discipline of history with the humanities because it is artistic as well as scientific and because it deals more with individual behavior.

History is the oldest social discipline, but it has many things in common with the rest. All seek to order facts into coherent sequences that may yield meaningful patterns, which in turn may reveal causal relationships. All study man, although history has to do more with uniquenesses and particularities than with similarities and uniformities. All recognize the problem of bias in the scholar, which arises from personal predilections or the "climate of opinion." Finally all seek to use the scientific method.

History differs from other social sciences in several ways. History studies the unique or nonrecurrent event resulting from individual action; other social sciences are more interested in studying the group to find predictable patterns. The historian is more concerned with studying the past through artifacts or documents, while other social scientists study the group more directly in the present through interviews, polls, case studies, questionnaires, and direct observation. Such methods may lead to general predictions concerning man in the future because of the uniformity that has often characterized human groups, but the historian eschews prediction and social control. The historian's vocabulary is less exact and technical than that of other social scientists. He seeks to integrate his material into factually based or in some cases moral generalizations that help him understand human action; other social scientists seek laws that can be useful in the prediction and control of human action. Both the historian and other social scientists must recognize that human nature is variable and not predictable in every time-and-space situation. In the final analysis the historian is more synthetic and other social scientists are more analytic in the ways they treat their data.

Discussion of each of the social sciences will usefully relate them to history. **Political science** is the scientific study of the theory and practice of human government to discover uniformities of political behavior and to formulate theories that can be used in the present. Plato, Aristotle, and Cicero were its main exponents in the ancient world. Jean Jacques Rousseau, whose deductive approach to government resembled that of Plato, and Montesquieu, whose inductive approach was more like Aristotle's, were its main practitioners in the eighteenth century when it became a separate discipline.

Political scientists now tend to divide on whether they should approach their discipline in such a way as to find principles for predicting and possibly controlling political behavior, or whether they should approach it in a more philosophical and theoretical way. History provides much of the data for political scientists, gives them perspective on the development of their field, and offers useful criticism concerning their theories in the light of the past. In turn political scientists help the historian refine his definitions of such words as *democracy* and of political institutions.

The Christian political scientist will look at all his data in a theistic framework rather than in the idealistic framework of Plato or the positivistic one of Aristotle. The state is for him an institution given by God, who has also imposed normative limits for it that are revealed in the Scriptures. Absolute sovereignty belongs to God alone, and both people and government are responsible to God as well as to each other.

Geography may be defined as the scientific study of man's spatial environment and his use of it, with the aim of discovering underlying uniformities. Environment is the static element and man the dynamic element in this definition, because man can modify his environment in many ways by technology. Physical geographers study the earth, climate, soil, and water, but human geographers study man's use of the earth in economic, demographic, and political geography.

Hippocrates, a doctor in ancient Greece, related geography to man's health, and both Herodotus and Strabo related geography to their work in other fields. Immanuel

Kant and Montesquieu emphasized the influence of geography on man and his institutions.

Geography helps the historian understand the influence of environment on human affairs without necessarily espousing the outmoded determinism that characterized the geopolitics of Adolf Hitler. Geography and chronology, according to Richard Hakluyt, are the two eyes of history. History may also help the geographer with its records of land use over the centuries.

Sociology, another social science, is the empirical study of present human group interaction to discover uniformities that may be useful to contemporary society. Except for those who are Christians, sociologists usually stress naturalistic and evolutionary patterns and consider man to be basically good and perfectible.

Sociology had its origin in the modern era with Comte, who coined the term and who wrote in *Positive Philosophy* (1830–1842) that man had passed through mythical and philosophical stages of his history to the present positive stage. In this stage he could through empirical techniques determine laws that would enable him to predict and control human nature. Man could then create a perfect order through human social engineering. Social work and urban sociology are applications of sociology to society, but without Comte's heady optimism.

Study of sociology helps the historian understand principles governing group action and social change. It also points to the family as the basic unit of society. In turn the sociologist has borrowed the principles of documentary study and the seminar technique from the historian.

Anthropology, one of the younger social sciences, studies scientifically the past and present cultures of preliterary man to discover underlying principles or uniformities that may have social utility. Like history it is a descriptive discipline. The anthropologist uses oral sources to study the past and observation to study the present, whereas the historian's sources are usually written documents or archaeological artifacts. Physical anthropologists measure and observe man; cultural anthropologists give more attention to ethnology, linguistics, and human archaeology.

Anthropology offers history the data from preliterary societies to link with the human story. It makes him aware of the possibilities for comparative study of cultures, a study like that of Arnold J. Toynbee. It has also laid to rest the theory of racial superiority that J. A. de Gobineau, Houston S. Chamberlain, and the Nazis developed, taught, and practiced. Unfortunately many anthropologists work on purely naturalistic and evolutionary assumptions that leave little room for a theistic approach to the data. This leads them to reduce ethics to customary, relativistic practices, rather than to base ethics on absolute principles coming from a divine lawgiver.

Economics is the scientific study of the production, distribution, and consumption of goods and services to find underlying principles of behavior that may be useful in the present and future. Plato classified society in his *Republic* along economic lines, but in the modern era economics is linked with Thomas Mun's mercantilistic ideas, Adam Smith's free-enterprise theory (developed in his *Inquiry into the Nature and Causes of the Wealth of Nations*), and John Maynard Keynes's ideas in the present century.

Economic studies have alerted the historian to the importance of economics as a contingent or conditioning cause in human history. The economist in turn gains much of his data from historical records and studies, and he finds that the historian can critically test his assumptions in the light of the past.

Psychology is the scientific, introspective study of individual and group behavior to find uniformities that help to understand man and fit him to his environment. Sigmund Freud helped launch psychology as an independent social science. Psychiatry has become an applied and experimental area of psychology devoted to healing the mind. Many psychologists are naturalistic in their assumptions, and in some periods they have tended to reduce man's actions to chemical reactions. The historian has found in psychology secondary explanations as to why men in certain circumstances react as they do.

The historian has thus provided the other social disciplines with data, perspective, methodology in some cases, and constructive criticism of their findings. He also integrates the findings of other social scientists into his account of the past. On the other hand, the social sciences provide the historian with general principles, some data for him to check and verify, more exact terminology, the comparative study of the past, and a better understanding of man.

If the social sciences rest only on a naturalistic, scientific foundation and methodology, and if their goal is laws that can predict and control human behavior, they fail to render full service to man. They must take into account the vertical, divine dimension as well as horizontal, human relationships. God is the creator of man and his environment and has given him such basic institutions as the family and the state. Human sin and failure can never be adequately explained by naturalistic assumptions and scientific methodology. It is man's tragic flaw that thwarts his efforts to achieve Utopia. These studies do, however, provide secondary data that the Christian can profitably study and use in the light of a biblical, theistic frame of reference.

The Fields of Historiography

History has scientific, philosophic, and artistic elements. No historian can avoid considering these areas if he teaches or writes history. History is scientific in method, in the accumulation of information about past incidents. The historian must criticize the documents from which his data comes by careful inquiry or research. Like any good *artisan* he must be accurate, impartial, objective, and honest, not withholding, changing, or creating evidence from his sources. He will then be able to answer the questions who or what, when, and where in connection with his information and even to make valid inductions.

When he has accumulated his data, he faces the question of why as he seeks to synthesize his findings into a coherent whole. He must take a broad view and seek to know and minimize his biases. At the same time he must recognize that he brings a *Weltanschauung,* a world and life view, to the task of determining the meaning of his material. This is the speculative or philosophic side of history, comparable to the *architect's* blueprint.

After accumulating information and linking it in a philosophic interpretation, the historian must consider how to impart or present his interpreted data imaginatively. This is the *artistic* side of historical writing, and it involves answering the question how. This literary reconstruction is an area in which historians have too often failed, ignoring the value of good writing in appealing to the ordinary man. Too often the historical monograph has left readers cold, so the average man has ignored history at great cost to himself and others.

The scientific, philosophic, and artistic aspects of historical study will form the basis of this work. Each will in turn be related to Luke's approach to history as set forth in the prologue to his Gospel. Past, present, and future elements are thus linked in any approach to history.

Annotated Bibliography

Several excellent studies deal with social and behavioral sciences and history. Berthold F. Hoselitz and others in *A Reader's Guide to the Social Sciences* (1959) give helpful definitions and describe the nature and history of each social science. Peter R. Senn's *Social Science and Its Methods* (1971) is a more recent book along the same lines. *Social Science Research Methods* (1950) by Wilson Gee is a helpful work on the nature of social science, its methods, and its relation to history. John H. Madge in *The Tools of Social Science* (1965) helpfully discusses techniques of social science.

Historians from ancient times have thought about and discussed their work. Polybius in his *Histories* devoted book 12 to a discourse on the writing of history, in which he attacked Timaeus for writing armchair history. Lucian wrote an essay in the second century A.D. on the theme "How to Write History." Ibn-Khaldun, the medieval Arab historian, wrote on this theme in the introduction to his history. Jean Bodin, and later Jean Mabillon, helped develop a methodology for historical research. Ernst Bernheim's *Lehrbuch der historischen Methode* (1889) became the law and the prophets to historians of the scientific school.

Several writers in the present have continued the tradition of writing books on historical craftsmanship. Gilbert J. Garraghan in *A Guide to Historical Method* (1946) covers the field of historical research and writing with a wealth of illustration. His balanced presentation takes into account a Roman Catholic theistic interpretation of history. Allan Nevins's *The Gateway to History* (1963) is an interesting and excellent literary presentation that covers all areas of historical writing and interpretation. His coverage of schools of history is excellent. Louis R. Gottschalk's helpful discussion of historical methodology in *Understanding History* (1969) has influenced the presentation of the author. Arthur Marwick's *The Nature of History* (1971) covers most areas of historical writing and study in a common-sense, practical manner and with clear illustrations. Contemporary sources on the issues of relativism and objectivism in writing history are provided by Hans Meyerhoff in *The Philosophy of History in Our Time* (1959). A helpful approach to the study, writing, and teaching of history is available in Geoffrey R. Elton's *The Practice of History* (1967).

Several writers focus on the actual writing of history. Robert J. Shafer in *A Guide to Historical Method* (1974) provides excellent coverage of historical method and writing. Jacques Barzun and Henry F. Graff in *The Modern Researcher* (1970) give down-to-earth guidance on aspects of historical research and writing. Homer C. Hockett in *The Critical Method in Historical Research and Writing* (1955) covers much of the same ground but with more emphasis on the writing of American history.

PART 1

History as Science

In the first four verses of the prologue to his Gospel, Luke very aptly summarized the essential elements of historical discipline. He discussed the scientific side of history in verses 1–3, the philosophic side in verse 4, and the artistic side in verse 3. His prologue compares favorably with those of the standard writers on historical method discussed in the bibliography of the introduction. Perhaps Luke's medical background made him more conscious of these aspects.

Luke discussed the nature of his materials in verses 1–2. He wrote in the first verse of the many who had written accounts or narratives of Christ's life, and he associated himself with them by using the words *us* (vv. 1, 2) and *also* (v. 3). He might well have had access to several secondary accounts of the life of Christ as well as to one or two other canonical Gospels.

In addition to these secondary accounts based on oral or written evidence, Luke had information from eyewitnesses about the life, death, and words of Christ (v. 2). He, like modern historians, valued contemporary, firsthand witnesses to history, or what are called primary sources. He had numerous opportunities in Caesarea and Jerusalem to talk to those who had been eyewitnesses to Christ's birth, words, deeds, and death. He lived with Philip the evangelist for several days (Acts 21:8–10) and lodged with Mnason, "an old [original] disciple" (Acts 21:16). Because the account of Christ's birth in Luke's Gospel is more detailed than the accounts in the other Gospels, and because it reveals something of Mary's innermost feelings (1:24, 36, 41; 2:19, 21, 51), Luke must have obtained his information about this event directly from Mary. As a doctor, he would have been a natural confidant for her. Like a good historian, Luke combined in his Gospel the best material from both primary and secondary sources.

He did not neglect historical method when transforming the sources into an accurate narrative. His doctoral skills helped him analyze the data. Luke claimed that he was writing his Gospel after "having traced the course (*parakoloutheō*) of all things accurately (*akribōs*) from the first" (v. 3 ASV). *Parakoloutheō* means "follow, trace, investigate a thing carefully." Paul used this word in I Timothy 4:6 and II Timothy 3:10, where it clearly suggests the idea of personal investigation and observation to obtain authentic knowledge. Luke investigated his subject "from the first" in the sense of time rather than place. His use of the adverb *akribōs* indicates that he was objective. He went on to say in verse 3 that his reconstruction of the life of Jesus was "in order," or systematic. No modern historian can quarrel with Luke's approach to his materials or his critical use of them to get the facts about Christ's life. In the next two chapters the material and method of the historian will be more fully discussed.

CHAPTER 1

The Historian's Materials

The historian must first collect his materials, whether they be artifact or document, before asking if they yield useful historical knowledge. He will usually find that documents from the ancient and early-medieval eras are too few rather than too many, because natural causes and wars destroy materials. He faces the question of whether these few documents are biased or atypical of the past. In more recent times an embarrassing wealth of documents has made the task of comprehending the whole story more difficult. This is the case with documents concerning World Wars I and II. The historian must also be on the lookout for forgeries. Most of his documentary evidence or testimony is indirect, so that facts come from it by inference rather than directly through observation (as in natural sciences like chemistry). Data from archaeology is an exception to this generalization. This primary task of collecting historical evidence is part of what has been called historical method.

Historical method may be defined as "a systematic body of principles and rules" to help collect materials, to analyze them critically, and to organize them into a systematic whole in the light of a tentative hypothesis. It is really a system of correct techniques for attaining historical truth.

Historical materials may be defined as human remains or the results of human activity that are meant to communicate historical information or that do so by their nature. Without relics, remains, recollections, and records the historian would be helpless, able to know only the present existential historical moment. Historians utilize documents to get information, and without documents there would be no written history. In the widest sense a document may be any written remain of the past; more narrowly, any manuscript or printed record; or in a still more limited sense, official papers from officials of the state or of an institution like the Roman Catholic church.

Primary Materials

Materials are classified either primary (original or source documents) or secondary. Source documents are underived, firsthand, or contemporary with the event. They are the products of an eyewitness either writing what he saw or heard or saying it (on such modern mechanical devices as television or audio tapes). It is not absolutely essential to use the original manuscript or tape if an underived, exact copy of the original is available. Some later printed copies of sources are more accurate than those closer to the original because of careful research and editorial comment. These firsthand sources are not so much valuable in themselves as for the credible facts that are in an authentic and genuine document.

Nonliterary Remains

Many historical materials transmit information about the past directly because those making and using them were unconscious of the fact that someone might use them to obtain historical information. These materials were made for everyday use with no idea of their being preserved for the future. Much of this material consists of archaeological artifacts. They are direct evidences of the past and exist apart from the historian's mind.

Architecture can be a helpful source of information to the historian seeking to reconstruct the past. The Parthenon in Athens, with the costliness of its materials, the beauty of its construction, and its size, helps one see how highly the Greeks of Athens esteemed Athena, the goddess of the state. The restoration at Williamsburg gives a clear picture of how the South's upper class lived in colonial times. The pyramids near Cairo graphically illustrate the important place death and the future life had in the minds of the Egyptians. Ruins of Ayutthaya in Thailand or Angkor Wat in Cambodia reveal the glories of the medieval kingdoms in Southeast Asia.

Monuments and statuary are also of value to the student of the past. The bust of Nefertiti (wife of Amenhotep IV), located in the museum in Berlin, helps one visualize the appearance of Egyptians in the days of the Old Testament patriarchs. Michelangelo's statue of Moses helps one understand the Renaissance artist's conception of the majesty of Moses as the Hebraic lawgiver.

Furniture is another record of the past. The throne chair, heavy gold coffin, bed, and chariot of Tutankhamen in the museum in Cairo help the historian reconstruct the Egyptian past. John Wesley's bedroom in London helps one understand the simplicity and sincerity of his life.

Pictures, whether mosaics, tapestry, painting, slides, or films, are also useful. Mosaics in the baths at Ostia near Rome, or those in the chancel of the church of San Vitale in Ravenna that picture Justinian and Theodora and their attendants, inform us of dress and art in that period. Neolithic pictures on the ceiling and walls of the Altamira and Lascaux caves are helpful sources of information for the prevailing view of life and the art of that age. Films of events or places are helpful if not tampered with by others.

Everyday implements, tools, and utensils also can impart historical knowledge. Lyres, fluted gold glasses, gameboards, and articles from Queen Shubad's boudoir at Ur throw much light on the third millennium before Christ. Scythes with wooden cradles, flails, and wooden forks are agricultural remains of use to historians. All of these functional relics of the past, though not designed or made to yield historical infomation about the past, do so because of their nature.

Literary Remains

Literary remains are usually intentional and conscious attempts to convey historical knowledge to posterity. With some literary remains, however, this is not the case; writing is sometimes incidental to the object. Even these remains, however, are useful to the historian.

Literary artifacts. Inscriptions of various kinds on statues or monuments are historical documents, the study of which is called epigraphy. The Rosetta Stone, with Greek, demotic, and hieroglyphic accounts of the same event, became the key that unlocked the hieroglyphics of Egypt. This document can still be seen in the British Museum. The inscription in Hezekiah's tunnel, which was quickly dug to bring water to Jerusalem during an impending siege, is an authentic document that confirms the tunnel's identification. Inscriptions of Queen Hatshepsut that were chiseled-out and replaced by later inscriptions of Thutmose III reveal the depth of animosity between these two persons. By 1880 thousands of Greek inscriptions had been collected and edited by August Böckh (1785–1867). Theodor Mommsen (1817–1903) did the same for ancient Latin inscriptions.

Coins can give the historian information on what materials people thought had value as currency, and they supply pictures of rulers and other prominent people of the times. Economic historians find coins to be a valuable source of information concerning economic conditions.

Some objects from the past combine pictures and words to give historical data, whether consciously or unconsciously. The Bayeux Tapestry depicts in picture and text the preparations for and the landing of William the Conqueror in England in 1066. The Roman catacombs with their pictures of fish, the ark, and the dove are of help to the church historian.

Manuscript or printed documents. These materials were usually intended to impart to posterity information about the past and therefore must be carefully tested for accuracy. They are usually divided into official and unofficial documents.

Official documents or public records are usually written by an official of the state (or of the medieval Roman Catholic church, which functioned like a state as well as a religious organization) acting in his public capacity. Most of these documents are preserved in great public libraries or national archives.

Archives, which in one sense are specialized libraries, may be maintained by states, corporations, or religious bodies. Some contain merely the records of a prominent man and are maintained privately. Much of their materials are manuscript or printed records. The National Archives of the United States was established by Congress in 1934 and opened for use in 1936. It now has nearly two million cubic feet of text, over 3,600,000 pictures, over 1,500,000 maps and charts, nearly 65,000 reels of motion pictures, and over 34,000 recordings. The Public Record Office in Britain performs the similar function of collecting and preserving state documents. Public archives contain records of state, church, or business, and private archives hold records of individuals that will be of use to the future. *A Guide to Archives and Manuscripts in the United States,* edited by Philip M. Hamer,[1] lists 1,300 such repositories and describes the holdings of each. Presidential libraries in the United States also serve as archives for presidential papers.

The Library of Congress is an example of a great national library. Copies of all copyrighted material have been deposited in this library since 1870. The Library of Congress was established in 1800 by Congress. Thomas Jefferson's 6,000-volume library was added in 1814 at a cost of $23,000. Herbert Putnam, after becoming librarian in 1899, helped bring the library up to its present level of excellence. Its system of classifying and numbering materials is used throughout the world in numerous libraries. Its cards and National Union Catalog are used by librarians to help classify and keep records for their own collections. The Library of Congress in 1974 had about 1,500,000 books and nearly 3,500,000 pieces, including maps, photos, records, and other kinds of material.

The British Museum also serves as a great national library for Great Britain, although many state documents will more likely be found in the Public Record Office. The Bibliotheque Nationale of France, founded about 1400 and now holding over four million pieces of material, is the national library of France and is a valuable source of documents for French medieval history. The Vatican Library, which houses documents of the Roman Catholic church, was begun by

1. Philip M. Hamer, ed., *A Guide to Archives and Manuscripts in the United States* (New Haven, Conn.: Yale University, 1961).

Sixtus IV in 1475 and now has between four and five million books as well as many manuscripts. It was not opened to scholars outside the Catholic church until 1881.

Numerous presidential libraries have been created to house documents, memorabilia, and books of individual presidents. These libraries, then, are also museums and archives. The first such institution was the Franklin D. Roosevelt Library in Hyde Park, New York. Others are the Herbert C. Hoover Library in West Branch, Iowa; the Harry S. Truman Library in Independence, Kansas; the Dwight D. Eisenhower Library in Abilene, Kansas; and the John F. Kennedy Library in Waltham, Massachusetts.

Libraries of our great public and private universities also have documents of value and interest to the historian. The library at Harvard has acquired over eight million books and pamphlets since its founding in 1638. Libraries at Yale and Michigan have valuable historical collections. The Hoover Library at Stanford University is noted for its collection of documents on modern international relations.

The New York Public Library, founded in 1895, is an example of an excellent municipal or city library. It has about eight million items in its collection.

Numerous private libraries also offer documents to the writer of history. The Henry E. Huntington Library of Pasadena is noted for its Tudor and Stuart documents, as well as for a fine art collection. The John Pierpont Morgan Library in New York has a wealth of medieval manuscripts. These libraries are usually supported by endowments from wealthy and influential men and are often named after them.

Such are some of the great collections of official documents. A fine discussion of libraries useful to historians can be found in the *Harvard Guide to American History.*[2]

An official *formal* document is characterized by a set pattern of words that is used again and again in similar documents. The Magna Charta of 1215, which the English barons forced King John to sign, employed much of the formal language of the era. Papal bulls follow a set pattern, as do laws of public bodies, resolutions, government bonds, and other formal government documents.

2. Frank B. Friedel, ed., *Harvard Guide to American History,* 2nd ed., 2 vols. (Cambridge, Mass.: Belknap, 1974), 1:36–41.

Official documents become *informal* when the official uses his own words rather than the set pattern. Communiques from military officers, reports from ambassadors or consular officials, minutes of committee meetings, tapes of phone calls, and diaries are all examples of this type of historical material.

Ever since the days of Leopold von Ranke, historians have often been too credulous in using this kind of material. Government officials may be dishonest, hoping to look good in the future and withholding or hiding unfavorable material. Government documents have to be tested with as much care as any other document.

Unofficial documents, whether formal or informal, are those of individuals unconnected with government or of corporations. Some of these are *formal* in that they follow a set form: e.g., parts of a will, a stock certificate, a bill of sale, and a lease.

Informal unofficial documents lack such a pattern. They may be public documents, such as newspapers like the *New York Times,* periodicals like *The American Historical Review,* chronicles like those produced by Puritan pamphleteer John Prynne, or films produced for historical purposes. Or they may be private, such as the diaries of Samuel Pepys and John Evelyn in the seventeenth century and Eisenhower's *Crusade in Europe* in the twentieth. Collections of private letters may also fit into this category. Most of the data used by the historian comes under the broad heading of literary remains.

Tradition. Intentional transmission of historical facts can be found in legends, proverbs, ballads, and sagas. These traditions may be oral or written, but they usually begin as oral testimony handed down from one generation to the next. Jan Vansina has done much to collect the oral traditions of the Africans in the former Belgian Congo by having the older men speak of these traditions and recording them on tape. Vansina has ably described the techniques for collecting this type of material in his *Oral Tradition: A Study in Historical Methodology.*[3]

3. *Oral Tradition: A Study in Historical Methodology,* trans. H. M. Wright (Chicago: Aldine, 1965).

Oral traditions often become written tradition. The story of Peter's crucifixion head-downward in Rome had evidently circulated for a long time as an oral tradition before Eusebius of Caesarea recorded it in his *Ecclesiastical History.* Aesop's Fables, Beowulf, and the Niebelungenlied are examples of sagas that were recited orally long before they were committed to writing. The historical accuracy of the Bible, which has so often been verified by archaeology, illustrates the way in which much tradition furnishes data that the historian can trust.

Living sources. Living persons who have participated in historical events may be valid sources of information through answers to questionnaires or through interviews by trained interviewers. After President Kennedy's assassination professional historians interviewed the people present at the time and recorded the interviews on tape. This material will be available eventually in the Kennedy Library. The tape recorder and the cassette have made this type of historical material more useful and usable. The historian, with the help of experts, has to make sure that the tapes have not been altered.

Secondary Materials

Secondary historical documents are derived from existing sources. They are written about people and events in the past by people in the present. There are several categories of secondary works.

Textbooks

Textbooks are secondary compilations of data from primary and often other secondary books. Textbooks in each field of history are written by experts in the field for use in public schools, colleges, and universities. A textbook is generally not as accurate as a monograph or cooperative work, although this depends on the expertise of its author. No historian who seeks to be fair to his topic can neglect the best secondary works by men who have used primary sources. Some textbooks, written by hack historians to earn money quickly, are nearly worthless.

Monographs

The monograph was developed in the seminar run by the great nineteenth-century historian von Ranke. It is an expert treatment of a limited field. Based on the study of original documents, it is fully documented with voluminous footnotes. The title usually expresses exactly the contents. Beatrice F. Hyslop's *A Guide to the General Cahiers of 1789*[4] is a monograph on the documents the voters drew up and sent by their representatives to the Estates General of France in 1789. Hyslop demonstrated from these documents that the people wanted representative government and redress of grievances by the king. Theses for advanced degrees are often monographs, as are many articles that appear in learned historical journals like *Church History* and *The American Historical Review.*

Cooperative Works

Sets that are edited by a general editor and that include articles by many specialists are cooperative works. The Cambridge History series for the ancient, medieval, and modern eras are prime examples. In some works the topics are arranged in alphabetical order. Sets like the *Dictionary of National Biography* of England give biographies by experts of important persons. Such works are more often used for reference than for casual reading.

These categories and examples of historic material show the wealth of materials upon which the historian can draw. He knows that a primary document is more reliable the closer it is in time to the original event. Because new material is being discovered, new techniques for critical study are being developed, and laws of evidence are being refined, a secondary book or document is more reliable the further it is in time from events described. We know that the fewer the eyes for whom a document is intended, the more likely it is to be accurate. Accounts by trained observers are more accurate than those by untrained observers. Unintentionally transmitted facts about the past in objects of everyday use are more likely to be reliable than facts transmitted for posterity. The historian will seek the best primary materials available and test them for bias, ignorance, and self-interest.

4. *A Guide to the General Cahiers of 1789,* 2nd ed. (New York: Octagon, 1968).

Annotated Bibliography

The author has found L. F. Rushbrook Williams's *Four Lectures on the Handling of Historical Material* (1917), in spite of its age, to be helpful in developing categories of historical material. Lucy Maynard Salmon discussed types of historical material in *Historical Material* (1933). She gave special attention to newspapers as a source of historical material in *The Newspaper and the Historian* (1923). Allan Nevins, Louis R. Gottschalk, and Gilbert J. Garraghan have excellent chapters on historical materials in their manuals on the writing of history. A helpful discussion on what archives are and how to use them can be found in Philip C. Brooks's *Research in Archives* (1969).

CHAPTER 2

The Historian's Method

After the historian has found the documents he wishes to study, he has much to do before he can derive historical facts from them. Documents are simply **statements of fact.** They are testimony, inference, or opinion about historical facts. The document may lack authenticity in that it is not the work of the person whose name it bears. It may lack integrity in that the text was later falsified through changes, additions, or subtractions. It may even be a false or forged document that contains no valid historical data. The Donation of Constantine was accepted as genuine for seven centuries before Lorenzo Valla demonstrated that it was a forgery.

The writer of history must give attention to historical method in collecting, criticizing, and classifying his material before he even begins to interpret or compose his findings. This is history as research or *inquiry.* The order of procedure is from document to data in the document. After finding his material, the historian tests it critically for errors of ignorance or for errors involving deliberate alteration or falsification of the facts. In all of this he will be as honest and neutral toward his historical data, whether artifacts, sites, or documents, as a scientist is toward his physical data. This is true whether the historian is a secularist, Muslim, or Christian. All follow the same procedure in obtaining facts from data.

The Collection of Documents

Historians have professional helpers in finding materials. The *archaeologist* provides material objects from the past that transmit historical information even though by their nature and function they were not intended to do so. He also provides documents on clay, stone, papyrus, or parchment that contain information about the past. The *archivist* is a specialist in the field of library science who collects, preserves, and catalogs manuscripts and early printed books. The *bibliographer* lists sources of information that guide the historian to the documents or information he seeks.

Bibliography

Finding adequate bibliography concerning the subject of research is the first step in the historical process. Full bibliographical details should be recorded on small cards. Three- by five-inch cards are used the most because they are just large enough for the necessary information: the author(s), translator(s), editor(s) or compiler(s) of the work; the exact title; the place and date of publication and the publishing house; the library call number in case one needs to use that source again; a full description of the book; and an indication of the book's value for the project at hand. Helpful sources for bibliographical information are the library card catalog; *The Publishers' Weekly: The American Book Trade Journal;* and the *Cumulative Book Index: A World List of Books in the English Language.* One should write on only one side of the card. The cards should be kept in alphabetical order by authors until it is time to organize them into categories and write the bibliography.

Building the bibliography and taking notes simultaneously will save many hours. Notes should be put on four- by six-inch cards or on half-sheets of typing paper. The former are more easily handled and will fit into a good-sized shoe box. Notes should be put on only one side of the card for easy rearrangement later. Only that which is relevant to the subject should be noted. Ideas rather than exact words should be recorded, except in the case of apt quotations. The historian can add in parentheses, as he goes along, any helpful thoughts or items of organization that occur to him. Modern techniques have greatly reduced the labor of taking notes, making it possible to reproduce mechanically the important parts of a document quickly and cheaply. At the top of each card should be the library call number, author, and short title of the source, and the subject of the note. At the end of the note-taking process, the cards can be rearranged in the order of the outline that has naturally developed while taking notes. Such a file offers flexibility in transferring data from one topic to another, and in expanding the number of note cards indefinitely.

Sources of Bibliography

Most manuals on method, such as Robert J. Shafer's *A Guide to Historical Method,* discuss the many types of bibliographical data available to the historian. These will help him locate material for his project.

Catalogs. Libraries have card catalogs that give full information about the books and their location in the stacks. Cards are arranged under the author's name, the book's subject, and its title; and if it is one of a series, it will be listed on a series card. Catalogs are arranged by either the Dewey Decimal or the Library of Congress system. Many libraries also have a shelf list in which the cards are in the same order as the books on the shelf.

There are also union card catalogs that list books available in several cooperating libraries. These books may be obtained by interlibrary loan or microfilmed for a small charge. For example, Wheaton College and several other colleges in the Chicago suburbs belong to LIBRAS. The books in the library of each college are on master card files located at each library. There are also union catalogs for libraries in given regions. *The National Union Catalog: Pre-1956 Imprints* of the Library of Congress lists books in 800 American and foreign institutions.

Printed catalogs listing the holdings of major libraries are also available. Two important ones are *The Library of Congress Catalog—Books: Subjects,* which is nearly 170 volumes in length, and the *British Museum General Catalog of Printed Books.* All copyrighted books in the United States and Great Britain have been deposited in the Library of Congress and the British Museum for many years.

Bibliographies. Bibliographies of bibliographies are valuable for leading one to bibliographies for particular fields. Theodore Besterman's *World Bibliography of Bibliographies*[1] lists 8,000 works. This volume led the author to Sidney Mendelssohn's bibliography of African history, which in turn led him to John Philip's *Researches in South Africa* (1828), an essential study of South African missionary history.

Historical Bibliographies by Edith M. Coulter and Melanie Gerstenfeld[2] is a useful list of bibliographies in the various fields of history. The *Guide to Historical Literature* edited by George Frederick Howe and others[3] is the best general bibliography for world history. The best bibliography for American history is the *Harvard Guide to American History* by Oscar Handlin and others.[4] There are several volumes of bibliography covering the field of English history. The bibliography of church history edited by Shirley Jackson Case[5] is helpful on material published before 1931 and can be supplemented by bibliographical articles in *Church History* since that time. Consultation of relevant bibliographies can save much time for the student or even the casual reader.

Indexes. Indexes of periodicals, newspapers, and books are helpful for those seeking valid information in those types of materials. *Poole's Index to Periodical Literature, 1802–1881*[6] indexes by subjects about 59,000 articles in nearly 480 British and American periodicals. Supplements to this index appeared through 1906. The *Reader's Guide to Periodical Literature*[7] gives subjects, author, and often title of articles in 135 magazines. It does for the twentieth century what *Poole's* did for the nineteenth.

1. *A World Bibliography of Bibliographies and of Bibliographical Catalogues, Calendars, Abstracts, Digests, Indexes, and the Like,* 4th ed., 5 vols. (Totowa, N.J.: Rowan and Littlefield, 1965–1966).

2. *Historical Bibliographies: A Systematic and Annotated Guide* (Berkeley: University of California, 1935).

3. *Guide to Historical Literature* (New York: Macmillan, 1961).

4. *Harvard Guide to American History* (Cambridge, Mass.: Belknap, 1974).

5. *A Bibliographical Guide to the History of Christianity* (Chicago: University of Chicago, 1931).

6. *Poole's Index to Periodical Literature, 1802–1881,* 2nd ed., 2 parts (Boston: Houghton Mifflin, 1891).

7. *Reader's Guide to Periodical Literature, 1900–* (New York: Wilson, 1905–).

Newspaper indexes open a wealth of primary material. The index to the *Times* of London and that to the *New York Times* since 1931 make available public opinion of the time on various issues one may be studying. Clarence S. Brigham's *History and Bibliography of American Newspapers, 1690–1820*[8] and *American Newspapers, 1821–1936* edited by Winifred Gregory[9] list what series or papers are available in which libraries or other depositories in the United States and Canada.

Perhaps the most-used and best-known index of books is the *Book Review Digest.* This work gives digests of book reviews that have appeared in about seventy-five American and English periodicals, furnishing the researcher with some idea of the book's contents and its value for his project.

Learned periodicals. Periodicals especially for the serious amateur and professional historian are available in most fields of history. *The American Historical Review* is the journal of the American Historical Association. It and most other journals in the field have in each issue learned and well-footnoted articles on very specialized topics, reviews of recent books, notices of meetings, and advertisements of new books. *Church History, The Journal of American History, The English Historical Review,* and *Speculum: A Journal of Medieval Studies* cover the areas described in their titles. *The Journal of Modern History,* published by the University of Chicago, is devoted to modern European history. Periodicals enable one to keep up to date with the frontiers of research in his field, new methods, new books, new documents, and professional meetings of interest.

Reference works. Encyclopedia articles written by specialists often give good overviews of given topics and helpful bibliography. They must be used with care, however, because errors often occur in them. The *Encyclopaedia Britannica,* particularly the ninth and eleventh editions, and *The Encyclopedia Americana* have many useful historical articles. These two encyclopedias are periodically revised and are supplemented with annual volumes. The older *Encyclopaedia of*

8. *History and Bibliography of American Newspapers, 1690–1820,* 2 vols. (Worcester, Mass.: American Antiquarian Society, 1947).

9. *American Newspapers, 1821–1936: A Union List of Files Available in the United States and Canada* (New York: Wilson, 1937).

the Social Sciences (1930–1935) edited by Edwin R. A. Seligman and Alvin Johnson[10] and the newer *International Encyclopedia of the Social Sciences* (1968) edited by David L. Sills[11] are both standard works, the newer one being more abstract and conceptual in approach. James T. Adams edited the *Dictionary of American History,*[12] which provides helpful data in that field. *The New International Dictionary of the Christian Church* edited by J. D. Douglas (with the present author as consulting editor)[13] provides information on topics related to church history.

Biographical data for deceased persons is available in the British *Dictionary of National Biography* and its American counterpart, the *Dictionary of American Biography.* These biographies are on the whole fairly accurate and are often quite lengthy. *Who's Who* in Great Britain (1848–) and *Who's Who in America* (1899–), a biennial publication, give biographical data concerning living persons of note. *Contemporary Authors* gives data about current authors. Each country has its equivalent to the various "Who's who" books, and there are specialized biographical dictionaries of persons in such fields as education, politics, and science.

Yearbooks like *The World Almanac and Book of Facts,* issued since 1868, and *The Statesman's Yearbook: Statistical and Historical Annual of the States of the World,* issued since 1864, as well as many others, provide useful information that is often otherwise difficult to find.

Atlases. William R. Shepherd's *Historical Atlas*[14] is still a good general historical atlas. The *Atlas of World History* edited by Robert R. Palmer[15] has excellent maps and text. Atlases of church history by Franklin H. Littell and Charles Anderson[16] (the latter atlas being more limited in scope) have

10. *Encyclopaedia of the Social Sciences,* 15 vols. (New York: Macmillan, 1930–1935).

11. *International Encyclopedia of the Social Sciences,* 17 vols. (New York: Macmillan, 1968).

12. *Dictionary of American History,* 2nd ed., 7 vols. (New York: Scribner, 1976).

13. *The New International Dictionary of the Christian Church,* 2nd ed. (Grand Rapids: Zondervan, 1978).

14. *Historical Atlas,* 9th ed. (New York: Barnes and Noble, 1964).

15. *Atlas of World History* (Chicago: Rand McNally, 1957).

16. Franklin H. Littell, *Macmillan Atlas History of Christianity* (New York: Macmillan, 1976); Charles Anderson, *Augsburg Historical Atlas of Christianity in the Middle Ages and Reformation* (Minneapolis: Augsburg, 1967).

clear maps, and the text helps explain the maps. Students of American history will find James T. Adams's and Kenneth T. Jackson's *Atlas of American History*[17] a helpful source of maps on various topics for the different eras.

Museums. Visits to museums give one a grasp of life during the period one is studying and a feeling of empathy with the past. Biblical history related to Egypt comes alive when one views the treasures of the Cairo Museum or of the University of Chicago's Oriental Institute. These artifacts were made not for the historian but for functional purposes and thus are credible testimonies to the past.

Historical sites. Herodotus's history of the Persian War is more colorful and interesting because he took the time to visit the important sites. Seeing the ruins of the Parthenon in Athens and the Forum in Rome have given the author a feel for the ancient world. Such an experience in the Forum inspired Edward Gibbon to write his classic work on the decline and fall of Rome. Historical imagination in reconstructing the past, if true to the sources, is decidedly in order if the historian wants anyone other than professionals to profit from his work.

The Criticism of Documents

The historian must test his documents by historical methods before deriving data from them. The average student or teacher will rarely have to do this, but the professional who finds new documents must subject them to criticism concerning the authorship and integrity of the text and the quality of historical testimony or facts in them. Historical criticism helps the historian weed out forgeries, falsifications, and errors; find out if the evidence is complete; and criticize his own ideas. Internal and external criticism help him know if the statement in the document is factual and if it constitutes valid evidence.

External Criticism

External criticism is the task of studying the document as a *statement* or *affirmation* of fact. The student at this

17. *Atlas of American History,* 2nd ed. (New York: Scribner, 1978).

point is concerned with the document rather than with the question of whether or not it contains historical facts.

Higher criticism. Higher criticism concerns itself with the *authenticity* or genuineness of the documents. A document's historical background is studied carefully, concentrating on its authorship, its date and place of composition, the reason for its writing, and its intended audience. Both internal and external evidence are studied for the light they throw upon these questions. Internal evidence is such things as the language and style of the document, but external evidence is the circumstances surrounding the writing of the document as derived from sources outside the document itself. Both historical and biblical critics borrowed much of their methodology from the earlier forms of literary analysis developed by German scholars.

Many special aids or auxiliary sciences are available to the student in his critical study of a document's origin. Diplomatics, first developed into a critical historical science by Jean Mabillon, analyzes the date of a document, its place of origin, its forms, the materials with which it was written, and its general style in order to establish its authorship. This includes special consideration of a document's invocation, the title of the sender, the receiver, the greeting, the text, and finally the conclusion. Different eras had stylized forms that are easily recognized by the professional and that help to establish chronology. Rolls, accounts, and charters from medieval times have been given particular attention.

The date of a document is important in assessing its authenticity. Eusebius of Caesarea in his "Chronological Canons," the second part of his *Chronicle,* put dates and events concerning the Jews in the left-hand column and the same for other nations in the right-hand column. His chronology was followed until Joseph Justus Scaliger (1540–1609) developed a more scientific one. Julius Caesar earlier had adopted the Egyptian solar calendar of 365 days in 46 B.C., adding a leap-year day every four years to keep the calendar approximately consonant with the solar year. The solar calendar still differed from solar time by a few minutes a year, however. Finally in 1582 Pope Gregory XIII made them conform to one another by declaring 4 October to be 15 October. This is why dates before 15 October 1582 in our calendar may be marked Old Style, and those after it, New Style. England adopted the change in 1751.

The seals on documents sometimes help to date them. The sender, after putting hot wax on the outside of the folded letter to seal it, would impress his seal ring on the hot wax to identify himself as the sender. The study of seals is called sphragistics or sigillography.

Genealogical investigation is also helpful in authenticating documents. Medieval families had coats of arms that can be used by the specialist in heraldry to trace lines of descent and relationships in families.

Numismatics, the study of coins, helps to establish dates, and the images of rulers that were often on coins give some idea of what these rulers were like. The ratio of gold or silver in the coin to the alloy in it can also help determine the amount of inflation at a given time.

Paleography, often considered part of diplomatics, is the study of handwriting in medieval documents. The paleographer also pays close attention to the ink used and to watermarks on the paper.

Analytical quantification of data with the computer provides additional grist for the historian's mill, checking general hypotheses and solving problems. Computers can be used to retrieve previously stored knowledge and analyze statistical studies. This can provide knowledge in several areas, as well as help demonstrate a document's authenticity. The computer is only a tool or instrument, however, because the problem of interpreting the computer data still rests with the man using the tool. This technique can be used to analyze voting data, population studies, wages and prices, census and tax records. It can also help develop checklists, concordances, frequency tables, and bibliographies. Philip D. Curtin of the University of Wisconsin used the computer in his study of slavery and came up with evidence that corrected many errors in commonly accepted views of slavery.

Both quantification and content analysis furnish internal evidence that helps solve problems of external higher criticism. Content analysis is a newer technique of quantification that also employs the computer and that helps determine the author of a document. The document is analyzed for recurring words, phrases, and ideas, then compared with documents whose author we already know, to see if it was written by the same man. Historians can also use this method to compare a person's actual patterns of thought with his patterns of thought as he sees them. Analysis of a politician's speeches is one example of this. Of course the researcher must be objective in pursuing his tentative hypothesis, following carefully developed procedure to avoid finding what he would like to find. Inference from such scientific study can be fruitful for our knowledge of documents and persons.

If one is studying the sites of old towns, boundaries of old fields, or mounds, aerial photography is a helpful instrument, especially if coupled with infrared photography. Older forms of agriculture and walls of medieval towns have been found in Britain through this means.

Psychoanalytic study of documents, done by one who is trained in both history and psychoanalysis, may be helpful. Documents known to be by one man may be psychoanalytically compared with other documents thought to be by him to help establish authorship. Such studies may also help one understand the subject's motives and actions. This method must be used with caution because one cannot put the person on the couch as a psychiatrist might do. One has only a few records of his feelings and ideas. Erik H. Erikson used this technique in his book *Young Man Luther.*[18]

One or more of these sciences or tools may be needed to provide valid data concerning authorship, date, place of writing, intended audience, and reason for writing. External higher criticism thus enables the historian to ascertain whether or not his document is authentic.

Lower criticism. Lower criticism, which follows higher criticism, concerns itself with the *integrity* of the document's text. Is the text in hand the original text? Is it marred by any later interpolations, additions, omissions, or even falsifications by later copyists or writers? External lower (or textual) criticism should answer these questions.

Distortion of the historical record is not an uncommon phenomenon. The text of a document may be incomplete or falsified for several reasons. Copyists of manuscripts can very easily make errors, which is why the courts are more interested in an original document than even a sworn secondary

18. *Young Man Luther: A Study in Psychoanalysis and History* (New York: Norton, 1958).

document. Copyists may also deliberately alter the text or make interpolations to change the meaning of the original writer. The Donation of Constantine was circulated for nearly 700 years and was used by the papacy to buttress its claims to land in central Italy. According to this document Constantine had given this land to Pope Sylvester I for healing him of leprosy. Valla in 1440, by carefully studying the text for anachronisms, showed it to be a forgery by an unknown person. Its use of the word *satrap* for Roman officials is one example of the anachronisms Valla discovered. The *Protocols of the Learned Elders of Zion,* which was written before 1900 and was in the collection of the British Museum by 1906, was used in Germany during the Third Reich and even in the United States to prove the existence of a Jewish plot to subvert the nations of the world and eventually to control the world. Jewish money power, corruption of morals through the press, and scientific expertise would enable a Jewish leader to dominate the world. Many supposedly authentic documents with textual integrity have appeared at one time or another to support such myths, and the student of history must be on his guard against them.

If numerous documents with slightly different accounts of the same events are available, the historian can profitably adopt the method used in literary and biblical criticism. He will find, after carefully comparing the documents, that certain of them are similar and constitute a group. Groups of documents may be linked into families. Comparison of families may lead to the conclusion that one document is the ancestor of the others and is the work of the author himself. This method has been used to put the text of the Bible on a sound scientific footing.

Determining the meaning of the text is another part of lower criticism. Is its prose to be taken literally or as poetic allegory with truth hidden in it? Semantics, or the meaning of words, is important because words are symbols whose meanings may change over the years. Grammatical study may also help establish the meaning of the text.

Internal Criticism

After the historian is satisfied that his document is by the man whose name it bears, that its text is identical to what the author wrote, and that the text constitutes an affirmation or statement of historical fact, he must face the issue of the document's *credibility,* reliability, or truth. Interpretation, inference, and opinion must be separated from fact in the document. What truth is in it, and what is it worth as historical fact? This is the task of internal criticism. At least four basic areas must be considered in determining whether or not the text contains historical facts that are credible.

What degree of *competence* did the writer of the document possess to report accurately what he saw or heard of the historic event? Was he close to the event in time and space? Was his health good so that his eyes and ears would function normally? Was his memory sound? Would his age or mental health have led him to forget the unpleasant facts or glorify his own role in the event? Errors of ignorance or inference could arise at this point. The matter of the writer's opportunity to report correctly is of first importance.

The writer's *character* or objectivity must also be taken into account. Did he want to please someone by his report, to exaggerate his part in the event to feed his vanity, or merely to indulge in propaganda? Could any benefit have accrued to him from the report? The intellectual limitations of his era might also have added a bias to his report.

The *context* of the document—the writer's mind-set and the climate of opinion in his era—must also be considered. This is the problem of subjectivity or distortion. If the writer holds a certain view of history, he might shade the truth in his report of historical facts. A Marxian will have a different view of the facts he observes than a Hegelian or a Christian interpreter will have. The historian must be aware of the writer's climate of opinion and of any personal or psychological biases that would color his report.

Matthias Flacius, a colleague of Martin Luther at Wittenberg, with the help of several others wrote a multivolume set called the *Magdeburg Centuries,* which argued that the papacy was the Antichrist. Caesar Baronius, a Roman Catholic, wrote a multivolume set called *Ecclesiastical Annals,* which pictured the Protestants as the disruptors of Christendom. Both used many of the same documents, but their respective mind-sets and the climate of opinion in their day affected their interpretations of facts. Charles A. Beard's preoccupation with the economic factor in history somewhat biased his study of the origin of the American constitution. In determining the amount of historical truth in a document, the historian must take these things into account.

Consensus of at least two independent observers or witnesses to the same historical fact is another test the historian uses. The biblical rule of two witnesses (Deut. 19:15; John 8:17; II Cor. 13:1) offers a good precedent to the historian. If two or more contemporary witnesses of a historical fact or event report the same information independently of each other, then their reports must reflect reality in past time and space. This is why such a high percentage of historical facts in textbooks can be accepted as truth. Other historians can check and verify a colleague's findings, so that over a period of years a consensus emerges on the basic facts concerning the past. The finding of historical facts in the statements of a document is thus the task of internal criticism, and the result is evidence about the historical event.

The Classification of Data

Classification or organization of one's notes follows the tasks of collecting documents and obtaining historical data from them. The researcher must digest his notes and arrange them under topics on the basis of at least a tentative hypothesis, though it is probably a verified hypothesis by the time he has finished collecting his information from the documents. This is the beginning of the work of synthesis, which follows the analytical work. One should not be so timid that he uses every bit of his notes to buttress his confidence, or so vain that he uses it all to demonstrate the profundity of his study. He will set aside anything that does not relate to the main thrust of his work.

Sometimes a chronological arrangement of the material is the most useful. Periods are handy pegs for the memory and set the bounds of the subject. Data can also be arranged by topics, by place of occurrence (i.e., geographically), by persons (biographically), by institutions, or by problems. In any case the organization should be logical.

The question of causation will arise as the writer arranges his data. He must carefully distinguish in his organization between secondary and primary causes. Extended discussion of synthetic interpretation of data will be given in chapter 5.

Is the historian then shut up to subjectivity as he interprets past events in the arrangement and writing of his findings? Consensus on basic facts can be achieved as his colleagues check and verify his data and conclusions. Both he and they will make use of scientific method and seek to be objective in their study of the past and the arrangement of their findings. Value-free inductions will come out of the data as the researcher amasses more evidence. The author discovered in his work on missions in Africa that missionaries such as David Livingstone in Central Africa and George Grenfell in West Africa put the Zambezi River and Great Lakes system on the map of Africa accurately. Both Christian and secular historians agree on this induction. The issue of meaning or interpretation of findings does raise the question of subjectivity. Causation in history is multiple and complex rather than simple and single.

Annotated Bibliography

The Use of Personal Documents in History, Anthropology and Sociology (1945) by Louis R. Gottschalk and others has a helpful section on historical method in the first seventy-five pages that is still relevant and has influenced this author. Robert J. Shafer's *A Guide to Historical Method* (1974) has a most helpful treatment of the matters discussed in this chapter. The student will find valuable the books by Jacques Barzun and Henry F. Graff and by Homer C. Hockett mentioned in the bibliography at the end of the introduction.

Quantification in History (1971) by William O. Aydelotte is a practical manual with examples of quantification involving the use of a computer. Some of Aydelotte's examples he took from his study of British electoral history and the Parliament of 1841. Samples of the best quantitative work were provided by editors Don Karl Rowney and James Q. Graham, Jr., in *Quantitative History* (1969). Ole R. Holsti in *Content Analysis for the Social Sciences and Humanities* (1969) defined, discussed, and illustrated the technique of content analysis. H. Stuart Hughes in *History as Art and as Science* (1964) has a useful discussion of the use of psychoanalysis in the study of historical documents to explain motives.

PART 2

History as Philosophy

It has been pointed out that Luke used the best secondary and primary materials he could find when writing his Gospel and that he claimed to have followed the best methods available in evaluating his material.

He insisted that he had sought certainty or truth (Luke 1:4) in order to present to Theophilus correct information about the life, deeds, and words of Christ (Acts 1:1). He wanted Theophilus to have truth concerning Christ rather than apocryphal tales or misrepresentations by Christ's enemies. No historian can have a higher goal than truth, even though he recognizes that the truth he finds will be partial and finite because he is a finite, fallible, fallen being. He cannot see the whole, no matter how extensive his research, unless he integrates truth from revelation with the facts in his documents. Luke believed that truth would help Theophilus live in the present and face the future.

A full discussion of the meaning or interpretation of the researcher's findings must include consideration of the classical writings of earlier historians. What historical methods did they use, and how did they impart meaning to their findings? Study of the great writers and books of history leads one logically to consider the various schools and philosophies of history that have developed through the centuries as historians have pondered the meaning of their findings. This search for meaning is an inescapable part of the historical process. If it is not done explicitly by the historian, it will be done implicitly.

CHAPTER 3

The Men of History: Ancient and Medieval

The historian has a tendency to mirror the civilization or society in which he lives. One usually sees the past in light of present needs, and when interpreting historical materials, one either explicitly or implicitly reflects one's cultural environment. Because of this element of subjectivity in the historical process, any study of meaning in history should include a study of how men have written and interpreted history in other eras. This and the next chapter are thus devoted to writers of history, their main works, their ideas, and the way in which they have been influenced. Carl L. Becker has aptly described this as the "climate of opinion."

People often forget that even before the advent of literary documents, there was history. This is now called preliterary history. The older term, *prehistory,* was really a contradiction of terms because since the advent of man, there has been history. Most of the data of preliterary history is furnished by archaeology and by anthropological studies of fossils and human artifacts. Although it may not be written, it is most useful to the historian because it is direct testimony from the past. Much so-called prehistory is in fact contemporary history in that contemporary primitive societies studied by anthropology differ little from those at the beginning of history.

Ancient Near Eastern Historiography

The supernatural and god-centered nature of historical writing in the ancient Near East is readily apparent even from a quick reading. The gods or God had an important part in human affairs in history. This was as true of civilization in Egypt and the valleys of the Tigris and Euphrates rivers as it was of Israel in the Jordan valley. These writers also believed that history has a didactic or teaching function, making morally better and wiser those who will read history. This wisdom might come from reading inscriptions or annals, notations of the important events of each year, or chronicles, factual annual records of the past. Archaeologists provide much of the material the historian uses in reconstructing this part of the human past.

Chronology is important in locating events properly in time. The Egyptians very early developed a solar calendar of 365 days, the last five days of which were an annual holiday. The Hebrew people developed the idea of time as points where great events, such as the incarnation and crucifixion of Christ, pierce time. Time was to them crisis as well as duration.

Egypt

When Napoleon invaded Egypt in 1798, he took along learned men to study Egyptian antiquities. An engineer named M. Boussard, while directing excavations for a fort at Alexandria, found what came to be known as the Rosetta Stone. Dating from the beginning of the second century B.C., the stone bore inscriptions in three languages, including Greek and Egyptian hieroglyphics. Working from the Greek, Jean Jacques Champollion (1790–1832) was able by 1822 to decipher the hieroglyphics on the stone and provide the key to reading all Egyptian hieroglyphic inscriptions. The stone is still on display in the British Museum, which obtained it from France in 1803 as part of an armistice between the two countries. The inscriptions on the stone were a record of the work of Ptolemy Philadelphus as ruler of Egypt.

Annals that name a year after the great event of that year and king lists are available from monuments. The Palermo Stone gives information about rulers of Egypt in the second quarter of the third millennium B.C. Manetho, an Egyptian priest, was asked by his ruler about 275 B.C. to prepare a history of Egypt, and according to Josephus, Manetho translated it "out of their sacred records" into Greek. This work was summarized and preserved by Julius Africanus about 200 B.C. and by Eusebius of Caesarea in the *Chronicle.* Modern historians derive from it the thirty dynasties into which the history of Egypt is divided. Documents written on papyrus, a paper made from reeds, also provide a wealth of material. From all of this, scholars like James Henry Breasted have produced accurate histories of Egypt and made available to us an abundance of primary documents they have copied off inscriptions on monuments and temple walls.

The Tigris-Euphrates Valley

History in the valleys of the Tigris and Euphrates rivers followed much the same pattern. The Behistun Inscription, chiseled on the face of a high rock by Darius I (521–486 B.C.), bore parallel inscriptions in Persian, Elamite, and Akkadian, the cuneiform script used by most nations in the area of these two rivers. Sir Henry C. Rawlinson (1810–1895), a British official assigned to that area, risked his life to copy the inscription, and in the 1840s he succeeded in deciphering the cuneiform. This made possible the reading of thousands of inscriptions and clay tablets in this script. Records of Sumeria, Assyria, and Babylonia were finally available to the historian as he reconstructed the past.

Berossus (300?–240? B.C.), a Babylonian priest in the court of Antiochus I, Seleucid king of Syria, did for Babylonian chronology in his *Chaldaica* (written in Greek) what Manetho had done for Egyptian history. Later archaeologists, such as Hugo Winckler with his discoveries of tablets at Bogazköy, the capital of the Hittite empire, opened the way for linguist Friedrich Hrozny to decipher Hittite writing. These discoveries have opened up chapters in human history that until the last century were only briefly mentioned in Greek classical or biblical writings.

Israel

Because of their bias in favor of the so-called scientific history, many historians in the nineteenth century minimized the historical contribution of the Hebrews or ridiculed it as "myth." Hebrew history in the Old Testament antedates that of the great Greek historians, whom these scholars lauded as great historians. The book of I Maccabees in the Apocrypha, which covers the intertestamental era, is also good history, as is Josephus's account of the first century of the Christian era. Jewish writers were among the earliest historians, and even prejudiced historians admit that these writers produced the first historical narrative with wide scope and "high relative accuracy." Fortunately the work of the archaeologist has helped confirm the accuracy of the historical writings in the Bible.

Hebrew historians were the first to have any real philosophy of history. Their development of a linear rather than cyclical concept of time and their consciousnes of the unity of the race under one God opened the way for such a philosophy. They also, unlike other ancient people, looked to a future golden age under their Messiah rather than to a past golden age. God as well as man is shaping history, in their view. History is a process that will come to a meaningful climax under the guidance of God. This approach gave a new perspective and wholeness to human history.

Flavius Josephus (A.D. 37–105?) was, apart from the writers of biblical books of history and the writer of I Maccabees, the major Jewish historian. He defected to the Romans during the Jewish rebellion (A.D. 67–70) and lived for nearly thirty years in Rome. He wrote *The Jewish War* and the *Antiquities of the Jews* in the mid-90s. The latter described Jewish history from creation to the twelfth year of Nero's reign; the former, the Jewish rebellion against the Romans in which the Jewish temple was destroyed. Josephus seemed anxious to justify the Jews and their faith in the eyes of the Romans, giving the Romans a better understanding of the Jews and their great past. He made wide and discriminating use of biblical and classical sources.

Both the Jews and later Christian writers thus possessed a linear sense of time that opened the way for spiritual and even limited technical progress. History is not just an endless cycle of existence from which man struggles to free himself, nor is it a march to Utopia by self-sufficient man.

Classical Historians

The Greeks

Secular historians tend to overemphasize the role of the Greeks in the history of history. The Greeks' greatest contribution is their critical approach to the sources, but this was by no means missing in the biblical writers. Thucydides led the way in developing a scientific methodology for the study of history. The Greeks, however, had a cyclical approach to time that put the golden age in the past and made the present and future degenerative and recurrent. Their attention was commanded not by deity but by contemporary man, living in the present, and his politics. They did hold that history is useful for imparting wisdom and instilling morality. Their historical presentation was mainly in narrative form.

Narrative historical writing made the Greeks think of history more as a literary than a scientific endeavor. Their childlike curiosity about the past led them to make careful observations before writing their histories. They also were curious about the why as well as the who, what, when, and where of events. They were mainly interested in contemporary history, because of which Thucydides and Polybius thought historical study would help make men wiser leaders of state. Their history was humanistic rather than philosophical or theological. They never succeeded in linking change or recurrent cycles in human affairs with cosmic permanence as the Hebrews did.

Greek history originated about 550 B.C. in Miletus, a city on the present Turkish mainland, where contact between Greek and Persian led to an interplay of ideas. These early Ionian historians, known as logographers, broke away from the poetic mythical writings of the early Greek past to write prose history from a more critical viewpoint. **Hecataeus** of Miletus (550?–478? B.C.) late in the sixth century wrote a work called *Genealogies.* He claimed that it was true history in contrast to the Greek histories of his time that he said were not only "numerous" but also "ridiculous." He tried to approach his task from a critical viewpoint to obtain truth about the past. Herodotus named Hecataeus as a helpful source for his own history of the Persian War.

Herodotus (484?–425? B.C.), often called "the father of history," wrote the definitive history of the war between Greece and Persia. He was born of an aristocratic family in Halicarnassus in Asia Minor. He was banished in 454, lived in Athens for ten years, and spent the rest of his life in a Greek colony in southern Italy. He was able to travel widely in the Mediterranean world to gather data.

He clearly distinguished in his history between what was based on hearsay and what he had seen and heard personally or had learned by inquiry.[1] He wanted to record the cultural as well as religious clash between the Greeks and the Persians and to relate how they had become engaged in such a long conflict. He used documents, interviewed many people, and visited historical sites—especially of battles—in gathering his material. He discriminated between what was more and what was less believable,[2] even though he loved a good story and included many that he did not believe. His somewhat skeptical approach comes out in several instances.[3]

This approach, indicated by Herodotus's use of the word *historia* in the sense of inquiry, was supplemented by his desire to produce a work of broad scope. To picture the great war adequately, he began by tracing the rise of Egypt and Persia on the one hand (in books 1–3) and of the Greek states on the other (in book 4). His work, which consisted of nine books, is unified by his picturing the conflict as one between Hellas and Persia, the West and the East, the Greek gods and the Persian gods. His approach is monistic, and he gave the gods more of a place in human history than did other Greek historians. Because he was a good storyteller, his work is more interesting than the colder, tighter narrative of Thucydides. Herodotus was more interested in *what* happened than in *why* it happened.

Thucydides (456?–396? B.C.) in his history of the Peloponnesian or civil war between the Greek states was more impartial and objective. He sought to find both immediate and remote natural causes in history, at the expense of supernatural causation. He thought the war came because Sparta was afraid of the growing power of Athens. He was as interested in the why as the what of history. His writing is accurate and somewhat cold rather than colorful and warm.

1. *Histories,* 2:99.
2. Ibid., 8:152.
3. Ibid., 1:182; 2:44; 3:3.

This is why many consider him the father of scientific history, notwithstanding his belief that history can make men wiser.

He was of noble birth, wealthy, and very experienced in political and military affairs. When the fleet of which he was admiral failed to save Amphipolis from falling, he was exiled from Athens for twenty years, during which he had time to study and think about the events described in his writings. What he had not personally heard or seen,[4] he took from contemporary witnesses after carefully checking the accuracy of their data.[5] He thought that poetic or mythical material is unreliable and practically useless to the historian because of partisanship or lapse of memory. He was less scientific in reporting speeches, admitting that he put into the mouth of speakers the words that his study led him to believe they would have used. His rigorous method led him to use only material that was relevant to his inquiry. He sought natural rather than supernatural causation in history, stressing the economic and political aspects[6] in his story of the conflict between Athens and Sparta. His history fulfilled the didactic function by informing military and political leaders on the wise course of action.[7]

Thucydides' history of the Peloponnesian War ended in 411, about seven years before the war concluded. Xenophon (430?–350? B.C.) finished the story in his *Hellenica,* which covered the history of Greece to 362. Xenophon was an excellent storyteller. His interest in people and his close observation of them resulted in the colorful character sketches that fill his book.

Polybius (198?–117? B.C.), the son of a general of the Greek Achaean League, was taken to Rome in 168 as a hostage to insure the good behavior of his Greek fellows. He lived in the home of the important Scipio family, mingled with Roman leaders, and traveled much in Roman provinces and colonies for twenty years. Interest shifts from Greece to Rome in his writings. His history of the period 264–146 B.C., the first truly universal history to be written by a Greek, was an inquiry into the reasons[8] why so small a people as the Romans of Italy had been able to conquer the Mediterranean world in such a short time. It is a fine analysis of Roman poli-

4. *History,* 5:26.

5. Ibid., 1:20–22.

6. Ibid., 1:24.

7. Ibid., 1:23.

8. *Universal History,* 3:32 (cf. 3:6–7).

tical ideals and military techniques. In book 6 Polybius attributed Roman success to a balanced constitution that judiciously linked monarchy, aristocracy, and democracy.

He was much concerned to do critical research in order to write accurate history. He attacked Timaeus, a contemporary historian, and set forth his own canons of historical method in book 12. If history is to have truth as its aim,[9] it must be written by men who have practical experience in war and politics, not by men who, like Timaeus, merely study documents and topography.[10] Research must be coupled with practical experience to produce the best history. Polybius was also concerned to write a universal history, speaking of history as a "connected whole," as "one piece," and thus linking the whole Mediterranean world into one history under Rome.[11] He believed that history can make men wiser by instructing them in past experience, and he pointed out that this is a less painful way to gain wisdom than is firsthand experience.[12]

Plutarch (A.D. 48?–125?) wrote biographical sketches of forty-six Greeks and Romans. He often paired together sketches of good and evil men, hoping to teach the reader to practice good conduct and avoid evil.

The desire to make their readers more moral and wise in behavior was frequently the motive of ancient, medieval, and even some modern historians until preoccupation with the scientific method made this motive suspect. Perhaps the greatest gain from Greek history is a critical, scientific approach to historical documents.

The Romans

Although the Romans conquered the Greeks, the Greeks captured the Romans culturally. The Romans fell under the spell of Greek culture even to the point of looking upon historical writing as literature. They also emphasized the teaching function of history. Their historical works were often less lengthy and more monographic in style and scope. They were primarily interested in contemporary history, to which the past was related as beginning. For the most part they used existing forms of historical literature rather than originated new ones.

9. Ibid., 1:14.

10. Ibid., 3:4; 12:25, 27–28.

11. Ibid., 1:1, 3, 4; 3:4, 32; 29:19.

12. Ibid., 1:1, 35; 3:4; 12:25.

Roman history began with **Cato** (234–149 B.C.) and his *Origines,* in which he discussed the origins of the Roman state. The only proper name in his book is that of Sirus, an elephant in the Roman army. Because history was useful to the state, Cato included a brief introduction in each book. He sought to describe past events with accuracy.

Julius Caesar (100–44 B.C.) in his *Commentary on the Gallic War* described accurately his military conquest of Gaul, but his interpretation of the facts was that he, an able general, would be a good political leader. For that reason one suspects that this work, though its military information is accurate, is a political pamphlet designed to influence the Roman people to make him their leader.

Sallust's (80?–34 B.C.) *Jugurthine War* and *The Catiline Conspiracy* are monographic in approach, focusing on a definite time and topic. Introductions concerning life or the writing of history begin each section and give Sallust's work a philosophic bent. His strong antisenatorial bias surfaces despite his intention to write an impartial account.

The rich and aristocratic historian **Livy** (59 B.C.–A.D. 17), a greater historian than Sallust, wrote his *Roman History* to glorify the ruler and the state. This prose epic describes the rise to world power of the little Roman tribal state. Livy's excellent style was described by George Byron as "Livy's pictured page." This well-planned work was really a tract for the times, written by a court historian to glorify Augustus the princeps. Livy wanted history to teach loyalty to the state and piety towards the gods. Only about a fourth of the 142 books of this work have survived.

Tacitus (A.D. 58?–120?) was the dean of Roman historians. In his *Annals* and *Histories* he did for the principate of the first century what Livy had done for the republican era. In the first he described the life, work, and foibles of the rulers up to A.D. 68, and in the latter, from 68 to 96. His writings reflect his dislike of these emperors and of their centralization of authority in the ruler, a process that helped destroy the republic. He believed that as men reflected on the way posterity would assess their work, they would seek to do what is morally good to enhance their posthumous reputations.[13] He even thought that history might go through moral

13. *Annals,* 3:65; 4:33.

cycles.[14] He tried hard to be accurate in his information,[15] but his idealistic view of German life in his *Germania* and of his father-in-law in *Agricola* caused people to suspect bias in his other books.

Suetonius (A.D. 75?–160?) also described the twelve Caesars in his *Lives of the Caesars.* While he, like Plutarch, had a moral purpose in these brief and fairly accurate biographies, it is sometimes obscured by his preoccupation with the scandalous and sensational in the lives of these men.

The reader will gather from this discussion that the Romans were not so much innovators in historical writing as they were imitators of the Greeks. Their admiration of things Greek led them—Livy in particular—to try to link Rome with the glorious past of Greece. History was for them mainly contemporary political history.

Biblical and Patristic Historians

Patristic historians found in biblical history a source and base for their view of history. They did not emphasize the rational side of life as the Greeks had. For that reason some, such as Sozomen, were too credulous in their descriptions of monastic life and miracles. They brought a new philosophical dimension into history with their sense of past, present, and future time as linear, not merely cyclic, and centered in Christ's incarnation or cross. Some New Testament passages suggest that there had been special providential preparation for Christ's coming to Bethlehem (e.g., Gal. 4:4); others, with their references to "the times of the Gentiles" (Luke 21:24) and "the fulness of the Gentiles" (Rom. 11:25–26), suggest special times of divine action in history. Through Christ a more personal element is acting in human history than impersonal fate, a more purposeful person than capricious gods. While these historians spoke of all men as one under sin, which is universal, they held out the possibility of a new humanity in a living organism, the church, which is the body of Christ and in which are those who accept by faith His atoning work on the cross. History has a teleology that is revealed in a divine plan during the course of history and that will be consummated at the end of history. Many of these writers were not clergymen, but all of them believed that the

14. Ibid., 3:55.

15. *Histories,* 1:1; 2:50.

study of biblical and extrabiblical history will make men better and wiser while they too make history and create culture. History for them has a sacred as well as secular side.

Luke's biographical history in his Gospel and the Book of Acts might properly be treated at this point, but this has been done elsewhere in this book. It should be clear from the prologues to his two books that Luke was in no way inferior to Thucydides as a scientific writer of history. Later Christian historians such as Eusebius, Socrates, and Orosius might well be the best representatives of Christian historical writing in the first five centuries of the Christian era.

The scholarly **Eusebius of Caesarea** (260?–340?) had access at Caesarea to the excellent library that Pamphilus had built, and after becoming a confidant of Constantine the emperor, Eusebius had the use of the imperial archives. His more irenic nature made him seek a middle ground in the dispute between Arius and Athanasius. His creed became the basis for the one that emerged from the Council of Nicaea in 325. The second part of his *Chronicle,* the "Chronological Canons," became the basis for the chronology of later Christian historical writers. In it he attempted to synchronize secular and sacred chronology by putting Jewish historical events in the left-hand column and those relating to pagan nations in the right-hand column; the dates he placed in a center column.

He is best known as the writer of *Ecclesiastical History,* the story of the universal church from apostolic days until about A.D. 324. He traced the church's advance from persecution and suffering to triumph in the days of Constantine, paying particular attention to the succession of bishops in the main churches of the empire, to martyrs, to heresies, and to events concerning the Jews.[16] He quoted many sources in "scattered memoirs," exercising some discrimination in his use of these materials and seeking to impart accurate information. Because of the variety of subjects he treated, his work at times seems to be more a collection of episodes than a unified whole. It is, however, our best source of information concerning Christianity during its first three centuries.

Descriptions of Christian history during the fourth century can be found in the works of **Socrates** and **Sozomen,** who were both laymen and lawyers, and of Theodoret of

16. 1:1.

Cyrrhus and Theodotus. Socrates was more impartial, used better sources, and was more accurate than Sozomen, who was credulous in his many tales of monks and miracles and who plagiarized much of Socrates' history. **Evagrius** continued the story of the fifth and sixth centuries with his long accounts of the various theological disputes.

Orosius (380?–420?), at Augustine's request, wrote *Seven Books of Histories Against the Pagans,* which he completed about 418. In it he sought to buttress Augustine's argument in books 1–10 of *The City of God:* Rome's calamities in the barbarian invasions were not caused by accepting Christianity and forsaking her old deities. Orosius's book, marked by blood, gloom, and doom, shows that many misfortunes befell Rome throughout her history and that after Christianity entered the empire, she possibly escaped many troubles because of the intercession of Christians. Orosius used history in this instance for a partisan apologetic purpose, but in the process he tried to write a universal history.

Medieval Historians

Medieval monks and priests continued the patterns of the earlier Christian historians except that they wrote in medieval Latin. In presenting the divine plan they discerned in human affairs, they were somewhat child-minded, employing a direct episodical style that left little room for literary padding. They emphasized the contemporary, and they saw in history a device to make men better and wiser concerning God and man.

Biographies of famous Christian leaders attracted many writers. Between 817 and 822 **Einhart** (770?–840) wrote a short life of Charlemagne. Because he was close to the emperor, Einhart described many of Charlemagne's personal characteristics, such as his love of Augustine's *City of God,* which he had someone read to him during his meals. Einhart did not neglect to give an accurate account of Charlemagne's life and work. **Asser** (d. 909?) wrote in the late ninth century in England a biography of Alfred the Great, setting forth Alfred's life and work as a Christian, soldier, and statesman. At about the same time **Jean de Joinville** wrote a *History of Saint Louis,* the story of the reputedly saintly Louis IX of France.

Most medieval historical writing took the form of annals or chronicles. In annals the main event or events of each year are listed beside each date by an author who, unlike the authors of chronicles, was always contemporary with the events he described. In chronicles the material was also arranged by years, but the accounts are more literary, more ordered, fuller, and often more interpretive. Annals are usually ecclesiastical and local in orientation, whereas chronicles deal with national as well as ecclesiastical affairs. The oldest annals are those of Lindisfarne, covering 532–973. Biographies, annals, chronicles, documents concerning feudal, court, and ecclesiastical matters, theological works, and direct evidence from still-standing monastic and church buildings constitute the main sources of information for the medieval era.

The Anglo-Saxon Chronicle and **Otto of Freising**'s (1113?–1158) *Chronicle of the Two Cities* are excellent illustrations of chronicles. **Bede** (672–735) wrote his *Ecclesiastical History of the English People* for the scholarly and practical purpose of informing the English about their conversion to Christianity and the rise of their church to 731. Bede obtained both oral and written sources and on occasion had copies of documents brought to him from the papal archives in Rome. He carefully distinguished between fact and rumor. His well-written history was for the "instruction of posterity," and his description of good and evil men was intended to encourage readers to imitate the good and avoid the evil of the past. Sometimes, particularly in books 4 and 5, his churchmanship led him to accept credulously tales of miracles by earlier saints.

William of Malmesbury (1090?–1143?) in his *Chronicle of the Kings of England,* written about 1120, described English history from 449 to 1125 in terms of the lives of the kings. He was impartial to both Anglo-Saxons and Normans in his use of sources available to him.

Gregory of Tours (538?–593), a busy bishop and traveler, also reflected in his account of the miraculous some of the credulity of the age. His *History of the Franks,* which covers the era from Adam to 581, is our major source of information about the Merovingian age and especially about the Franks becoming loyal sons of the medieval church. Dialogue, digressions, and tales help to make the work interesting. Gregory "commemorated the past" in order to bring it "to the knowledge of the future." He believed that God providentially controls history.

Others wrote chronicles of the Crusades. **Foucher of Chartres** (1058–1127?), author of *The History of the Crusades,* was an eyewitness who accompanied Baldwin as a chaplain. Foucher pictured the crusaders doing the will of God, even when slaughtering the enemy in battle. Miraculous events are a part of Foucher's narrative. **William of Tyre** (1130?–1193?) in his *History of Jerusalem* and **Geoffroi de Villehardouin** (1167?–1213?) in his chronicle of the fourth crusade took a similar approach to the subject.

Jean Froissart (1333?–1404?) wrote a chronicle that listed events in the histories of France, England, Spain, and Scotland from 1325 to 1400. His description of the Hundred Years' War stresses the chivalrous side of feudal war. **Ordericus Vitalis** (1075–1143?), a French monk, wrote his *Ecclesiastical History* after much travel and careful, original research. He approached his task of describing the story of the French church with a moralistic motive.[17]

Procopius (500?–565?), who lived in the eastern empire, wrote the *History of the Wars* and the *Secret History* in Greek rather than the prevailing Latin. The first is a polished account of the Byzantine Empire and of the emperor Justinian's reconquering the west from the barbarian invaders. Procopius's interest was in the aristocracy and the civilizing work of the empire. His second work describes palace intrigue and moral debauchery in Constantinople.

Ibn-Khaldun (1332–1406) well represents Muslim historiography. In his *Muqaddimah* (1377), a seven-volume history of the Berber and Muslim dynasties in North Africa, he set forth his ideas about the materials, method, and meaning of history. He believed that impartial critical investigation of primary data will yield truth, and that history is empirical and scientific. He did not forget to state that all of history proceeds under the watchful eye of Allah. He held a psychocultural view of history according to which a strong people spoiled by success and soft living lose their initial drive and fall before another group. He gave attention to geographic, psychological, economic, and social factors in describing these cycles.

17. 5:1; 6:1; 9:27.

Most medieval history was written in monastery libraries, royal courts, and cathedral libraries. Many modern historians fault medieval writers for their attention to the supernatural, but these critics ignore the manner in which these medieval historians sought firsthand sources and checked them critically with information accessible through the simpler methods of their times. Medieval writers did recognize their presupposition that history is unified and controlled by Providence, a presupposition that helped make history meaningful and instructive in the present. Historians in the Renaissance and Enlightenment utilized more critical methods, but they, like their medieval predecessors, had an implicit if not explicit philosophy of history to help them extract meaning from the data. Perhaps historians today, without forsaking scientific methodology in establishing facts, could well afford to give attention to the providential element in history when interpreting what they have discovered.

Annotated Bibliography

Several good manuals cover the history of history, which is the subject of this and the next chapter. Although it is written from an antisupernatural viewpoint that assumes social as well as biological evolution, Harry E. Barnes's *A History of Historical Writing* (1963) has helpful, factual discussions of the times, life, and writings of major historians. *The Heritage and Challenge of History* (1971) by Paul K. Conkin and Roland N. Stromberg surveys the history of history. Part 1 of Noah E. Fehl's *History and Society* (1964) includes both a survey and a study of the sources of history. *The Development of Historiography* (1954), edited by Matthew A. Fitzsimons, Alfred G. Pundt, and Charles E. Nowell, although a survey of the history of history, has a detailed treatment of twentieth-century and American historiography. Michel François and others in *Historical Study in the West* (1968) offered a helpful survey of the field, with special chapters on history in France, West Germany, Great Britain, and the United States. James Westfall Thompson's and Bernard J. Holm's *A History of Historical Writing* (1942) is detailed and includes a wealth of material.

The History of History (1939) by James T. Shotwell (in this first volume of a still-incomplete series) discusses historical writers and writing of the ancient world, and it includes some church historians. Michael Grant in *The Ancient Historians* (1970) ably covered both pagan and Christian historians of the ancient world. Max L. W. Laistner's *The Greater Roman Historians* (1947) is helpful in the field of Roman historiography. John B. Bury's *The Ancient Greek Historians* (1909) can still be used with advantage in studying ancient Greek historiography.

The work of early church historians is ably discussed by Frederick J. Foakes-Jackson in *A History of Church History* (1939). In chapters 2 and 3 of *Luke: Historian and Theologian* (1970), I. Howard Marshall discussed Luke as an able historian. Robert L. P. Milburn in *Early Christian Interpretations of History* (1954) covered somewhat the same ground as Foakes-Jackson. Henry W. Bowden's *Church History in the Age of Science* (1971) contains helpful accounts of the work of modern church historians like Philip Schaff, John D. G. Shea, Ephraim Emerton, and others.

CHAPTER 4

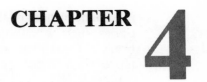

The Men of History: Modern

Between 1350 and the present, the purpose of writing history shifted from making men wiser and more moral to helping them think about the past and satisfy their curiosity. Approached along scientific lines, history became more humanistic, giving less attention to the role of God in human affairs.

Historians of the Renaissance (1350–1517)

Although Renaissance tendencies persisted particularly in northwestern Europe until 1648, the major activities of Renaissance historians were completed before the Reformation began under Martin Luther. Reformation historians broke sharply with those of the Renaissance.

Medieval and Reformation historians were deeply interested in the Christian past, but Renaissance writers were more interested in the history of Greece and Rome. Scholars vied with each other in finding and critically studying classical documents. Collections of such documents were amassed by merchant princes of the Italian city-states and by Renaissance popes, such as Nicholas V, who founded the great Vatican Library. Humanistic secular studies interested these scholars more than theology, so their writings tend to be man-centered. Historical writing usually focused on local matters and the development of Italian city-states. Most of these writers were laymen with practical experience in business or politics, but they were above all humanists who deeply loved the literature of Greece and Rome.

Advances of long-term value in critical historical methodology were made in this era. **Joseph Justus Scaliger** (1540–1609) in 1583 wrote *The Restoration of Chronology,* in which he revised the chronology of Eusebius of Caesarea. While Eusebius had emphasized the Jewish nation, Scaliger gave more attention to the history and chronology of surrounding pagan nations. This made Scaliger's chronology more scientific than that of Eusebius.

Lorenzo Valla (1406–1457) deserves much credit for his accomplishment in the field of textual criticism. He had at one time been a papal secretary, and in 1440 when he began to serve Alphonse, king of Aragon and Sicily, he wrote *The Discourse of Lorenzo Valla on the Forgery of the Alleged Donation of Constantine.* The document known as the Donation of Constantine was first circulated widely about 756, when the Frankish ruler Pepin III granted some land in central Italy to the papacy and used the document to buttress his gift. According to the Donation of Constantine, the emperor, in gratitude for having been healed from leprosy by the bishop of Rome, Sylvester I, gave the bishop royal regalia, a palace in Rome, and land in Italy. This document was cited as genuine for nearly seven centuries until Valla exposed it as a forgery by careful study of internal evidence, particularly anachronisms in the text. The use of the word *satrap* as the title of Roman officials was obviously incorrect, Valla pointed out; *satrap* had been the title of governors in the old Persian Empire.

Jean Bodin (1530–1596) also wrote concerning historical method in *Method for the Easy Comprehension of History* (1566). He pondered the problems of historical interpretation, stressed the importance of geography, and developed a doctrine of progress similar to that of many modern historians. The honest historical criticism of the Bollandist

Fathers, a group of Jesuit scholars, continued and refined this critical outlook.

There were many Italian historians of note in this era, and **Niccolò Machiavelli** (1469–1527) was the greatest of them. As a diplomatic and civil servant in Florence, he had much to do with foreign policy and traveled extensively in the course of his work. Then because of a shift in Italian politics, he was exiled from Florence. At the request of Clement VII (Giulio de' Medici), Machiavelli wrote a *History of Florence* (1525), in which he abandoned a supernaturalist approach to history for humanistic and materialistic causation. He did relate foreign policy and domestic affairs better than previous historians had done. He hoped the Italian city-states would unite under a strong ruler who could stop Spanish and French interference in Italy's affairs.

Historians of the Reformation (1517–1648)

Historical writers during the Reformation worked within an entirely different frame of reference than those of the Renaissance. They turned from a more objective, secular history to a subjective, theological, God-centered approach, similar to that of Augustine and Orosius. Although they obtained firsthand sources, criticized them carefully, and cited them fully, they wrote history that was argumentative and passionately partisan, intending to discredit their religious opponents and validate their own place in the historical succession.

John Foxe (1516–1587) in 1563 published his multivolume work, *Acts and Monuments of These Latter and Perilous Days* (or, *The Book of Martyrs*), to show how the papacy had always persecuted those who stood for a biblical faith. He seems to suggest that in his era Queen Elizabeth I of England, the Anglican Church, and the English people were the elect who would withstand all the wrath of the papacy in order to establish an earthly kingdom of God.

Matthias Flacius (1520–1575), or as he is known by the latinized form of his name, Flacius Illyricus, taught Hebrew at the University of Wittenberg. He bitterly disliked the papacy, so with the help of six colleagues he produced the thirteen-volume *Magdeburg Centuries* (1559–1574), a work that attempted to show that the pope was the Antichrist and a perverter of biblical truth. It was well-documented because the author had collected numerous primary sources, but his interpretation of the data was very partisan and bitter.

Caesar Baronius (1538–1607) did for Roman Catholicism what Flacius had done for Protestantism. At the request of Philip of Neri, his superior in the Oratorian Order, Baronius delved into the resources of Italian and Vatican libraries for thirty years to gather data for and to write his twelve-volume *Ecclesiastical Annals,* a reply to Flacius. Baronius wanted to show that the Roman Catholic faith and church had been "always the one and same," that it had been pure even when troubled by "changes of events and times," and that papal authority was legitimate.

John Sleidan (1506?–1556) wrote a much more impartial and factual analysis of the Reformation, despite his tendency to favor the Lutheran states. **John Knox** (1505–1572) in his *History of the Reformation of the Church of Scotland* (1644) avoided consciously falsifying data or suppressing facts, even though he favored the Protestant movement in his homeland.

Historians of the Enlightenment (1648–1789)

The supernatural world and life view of the Middle Ages was continued to some extent in the Reformation but began to dissolve during the Enlightenment. Earlier discoveries and colonial and imperial expansion in Africa, Asia, and North and South America stimulated the imagination as Europeans came into contact with new people, religions, and customs. Marco Polo's book about his sojourn in China and Richard Hakluyt's series of books on travel and exploration sold widely.

The seventeenth-century scientific revolution resulted in an emphasis on natural law, which can be discovered by human reason. Discoveries in pure science, such as Sir Isaac Newton's formulation of the law of gravitation, led people analogically to think that reason accompanied by scientific method could bring indefinite progress for man, who is perfectible. Deism was simply natural law applied to religion, the formulation of a natural religion common to all men. According to Deism, an absentee creator God should be worshiped now by an ethical life in order to enjoy reward rather than punishment in a future life.

This secular, skeptical, anticlerical climate of opinion strongly influenced historians of the day. Although anthropocentric, optimistic, and rationalistic, they retained the Christian concept of a future golden age and a teleological approach to history. They secularized it, however, and so were unfair to Christian historians. They turned from episodic supernatural history to broad, sociocultural history, which for the first time sought to describe a whole civilization. Voltaire did this in *The Age of Louis XIV* (1751). Giovanni Battista Vico and others developed a natural-law philosophy of history that either ignored or inverted the supernatural. They looked for an earthly millennium that would result from the inevitable progress of perfectible man, aided by science. They substituted faith in the secular dream of progress for faith in Providence. While they were critical in the handling of sources, they could not rise above the presuppositions of their system of interpretation.

Voltaire's (1694–1778) ***Age of Louis XIV*** **provides** the best illustration of this new history of civilization. He carefully gathered 100 volumes of printed memoirs over the twenty-year period during which he prepared and wrote his history. He claimed to be writing "the history of the human mind" in "the most enlightened century that ever was" rather than a mere biography of Louis XIV. This great French culture would move to ever-increasing perfection. Voltaire saw history as a whole, and using a topical approach, he placed the reader in the midst of seventeenth-century French civilization. He had a prejudice against war and against the Roman Catholic church, which he thought should be crushed. Voltaire was also the first to coin the term "philosophy of history," although his main work is not a philosophy of history.

Edward Gibbon (1737–1794) in *The History of the Decline and Fall of the Roman Empire* (1776–1788) did for Roman civilization what Voltaire had done for French culture. Gibbon's early studies, pursued at home until he was sixteen because he was frail and ill, were encouraged by Katherine Porten, his aunt. He spent most of his time at the Oxford University library in desultory reading. Fortunately, during a residence in Switzerland from 1753 to 1758, Daniel Pavillard taught Gibbon how to study systematically. His **father's annual settlement upon him finally made him financially** independent. He labored for twenty years to gather materials and write his great history. The vision of this task came while viewing the ruins of the Roman Forum on 15

October 1764 and pondering how and why imperial Rome had come to such a sorry state. Gibbon obtained the best printed sources, but he expressed his interpretation of the facts with such loaded words as "disgusting" and "grafting and profligate." His deistic, rationalistic presuppositions rendered him incapable of understanding Christianity, so that he attributed the downfall of Rome to "the triumph of barbarism and Christianity."

Gibbon did not forget the Byzantine Empire in his polished literary presentation. After finishing the story of the western empire in the fifth century, he continued in less detail the story of Roman culture at Constantinople from 641 to 1453, when the city fell to the Turks. Because Gibbon's work reflected the deistic outlook of the English upper class, it was widely read and earned him nine thousand pounds.

Christoph Kellner (1634–1717) in this same era provided the framework of historical chronology. He divided history into ancient, medieval, and modern periods, although he did it in a patronizing manner that made his era the climax of history.

Jean Mabillon (1632–1707) furthered the study of external criticism by publishing *De re diplomatica* (1681). He claimed to have formulated rules "for distinguishing genuine manuscripts from those that are false and interpolated." Thus he founded the science of external higher criticism to deal with the materials of diplomatics, such things as forms, seals, paper, ink, and handwriting. He wrote this fine work to refute a Jesuit pamphlet and prove the authenticity of the charters of the abbey of St. Denis. Since Mabillon's day diplomatics has been a highly skilled auxiliary discipline that helps the historian with his sources.

Historians of the Romantic Era (1789–1850)

Perhaps the excesses of the French Revolution, all in the name of reason, made people tired of the overemphasis on rationality and the scientific approach. Beginning in Germany, an emphasis on the emotional, mystical, or imaginative side of life and the importance of the individual replaced a cold, rational outlook. The lake poets of England in literature, Jean Jacques Rousseau in political science, and Georg Hegel and other idealists in philosophy reflected the new spirit of the age, or what they called the *Zeitgeist*.

This atmosphere created an interest in biographical history like that of Thomas Carlyle. It also promoted glorification of the nation and patriotism in the writings of such men as Jules Michelet in France, George Bancroft in the United States, and Heinrich von Treitschke in Germany. Scholars in Germany began the practice of creating national archives, in which documents of the nation's past are housed. Writers such as Immanuel Kant, Johann Gottfried von Herder, and especially Hegel became the first since Augustine and Otto of Freising to formulate a philosophy of history. Hegel emphasized the evolutionary development of the nation, controlled by an absolute that is seeking to manifest itself in human history. *Development, evolution,* or *growth* became a key word for the historian.

Jules Michelet's (1798–1874) *History of France,* seventeen volumes published from 1833 to 1867, well illustrates romantic historiography. While Michelet sought to be scientific in obtaining his facts, he interpreted French history as the "drama of human liberty" after the revolution in 1789. He loved France, her "people," and her new-found democracy, and he was anticlerical in his outlook.

Thomas Carlyle (1795–1881) of England revealed his contempt for the masses and his biographical approach to history in his *On Heroes, Hero-Worship, and the Heroic in History,* published in 1841. History to him is only collective biography, "the history of great men who have worked here." For this reason his writing is subjective and moralistic. **John L. Motley** (1814–1877), who recorded the heroic rise of the Dutch republic; **Francis Parkman** (1823–1893), who fought the threat of blindness while writing about the role of the French and Indians in the early colonial history of North America; and **George Bancroft** (1800–1891), who was a nationalistic and subjective chronicler of the rise of the United States—all were a part of this romantic mode of historiography. Nor should one forget **Thomas B. Macaulay**'s (1800–1859) five-volume *History of England from the Accession of James II,* with its fine literary style and pro-Whig bias for William of Orange.

Romanticism also promoted, as has been mentioned, the rise of national archives. **H. F. Karl** (1757–1831), or Baron von Stein, who led Prussia in her struggle against Napoleon, patriotically raised money to form a society to collect the documents of early German history. **Georg H. Pertz** (1795–

1876) from 1823 and later **Georg Waitz** (1813–1886) until 1875 worked as editors to collect and edit the ancient and medieval sources of German history. The 120-volume *Monumenta Germaniae Historica* was finally completed in 1925. **François Guizot** (1787–1874) in 1833 organized in France the Society of French History to collect, edit, and publish the source papers of that nation's early history. Since that time nearly 300 volumes of French documents have been published. **William Stubbs** (1825–1901) edited many of the 243 volumes of English medieval documents in the Rolls Series (*Chronicles and Memorials of Great Britain and Ireland During the Middle Ages*), published between 1858 and 1911. In the United States the Library of Congress was founded in 1800 and became a depository of many important historical documents. These national archives reflected historians' romantic preoccupation with the nation in this era.

Modern Scientific Historians (1850–)

The scientific method and the universities of Germany had a marked influence on the writing of history in the late nineteenth century. Many historians agreed with John B. Bury's idea that history is "a science, no less and no more." Facts were almost worshiped because of the belief that if one could get all the historical facts, one could reconstruct the past exactly. Historical writing and teaching became the vocation of professionals rather than the avocation of wealthy men, and it found a congenial home in the universities. Professional societies such as the American Historical Association were organized.

Although Leopold von Ranke became the patron saint of academic, positivistic (or scientific) historians, particularly in America, the Dane **Barthold G. Niebuhr** (1776–1831), professor of history at the University of Berlin, promoted the scientific study of history in seminars before von Ranke did. In seminars students could engage in critical study of the sources under master historians.

Leopold von Ranke (1795–1886), who thought of himself as both a historian and a Christian, was the primary leader in developing the idea that history is a science. Von Ranke, who first became interested in history in high school, obtained his Ph.D. at Leipzig at an early age, writing his dissertation on the work of Thucydides. While teaching classical languages at Frankfurt, he studied Sir Walter Scott's *Quentin Durward* and became aware that the Louis XI and Charles the Bold pictured there never existed in historical fact. From this point he turned to the study and teaching of history, becoming a professor at the University of Berlin in 1825. By 1833 he had founded his historical seminar, in which over a hundred scholars would receive their historical training.

Von Ranke made truth, obtained by gathering the facts from historical documents, the *motivation* for all historical work. He wanted history to be "*wie es eigentlich gewesen*" (as it actually happened), or in modern parlance, to "tell it like it was." "The strict presentation of facts" was to him "the supreme law of historical writing." Only then could one have "exposition of the unity and progress of events."

A lengthy stay in Venice, where von Ranke used the governmental archives, convinced him of the value of such archives. He also visited archives in Vienna, Paris, and Rome. He became convinced that the best *materials* for historical study are documents from governmental archives. History should be written, he believed, from eyewitness accounts, which are the "purest, most immediate documents." Von Ranke forgot in his overly optimistic evaluation of government documents that officials do not always present the truth. Sometimes they slant their writings for various reasons, and sometimes they will even change the facts, as Otto von Bismarck did in the Ems Telegram, for reasons of state.

The historical seminar, in which a master historian guides students in their study of primary documents and criticizes their efforts at internal criticism of the documents, was in von Ranke's opinion the best *method* to train future historians. He borrowed this technique from philologists who used it in literary textual criticism. His American students enthusiastically introduced this method into the universities of their country. Von Ranke had his students present the fruit of their studies in *monographs,* which dealt with a detailed subject, had an exact title, and were carefully documented.

Many worshipers of von Ranke and his approach forgot that in spite of his scientific approach, he did interpret his facts in a theistic framework, so that history became "a revelation of God." He thus linked the empirical approach with philosophical interpretation. He thought that history is a synthesis of human effort and God's will, not the outworking of natural or mechanical forces. All eras of history are "immediate to God," who wills and controls history through a cosmic plan. Few historians have had the influence on their students that von Ranke had.

Henry T. Buckle (1821–1862) was even more positivistic than von Ranke. He believed not only that the study of history should be scientific in method, but also that it should lead to the formation of uniformities or historical laws. Fustel de Coulanges in France and Henry Brooks Adams in the United States were also interested in finding laws in historical data that would have as much validity as those in the more exact sciences.

The scientific historians notwithstanding, historical writing is influenced by the climate of opinion. Another example of this phenomenon is the research, conducted in the 1920s, into the causes of World War I. At the beginning of the war various governments issued so-called "rainbow books" to show that one of the powers on the other side was guilty of starting the war. Shortly after the war the Russian Communist and the German socialist governments opened their wartime archives and published documents to discredit their monarchical predecessors, and this forced the Allies to do the same. Normally these documents would not have become accessible to scholars until all the participants had died.

The writer, while a graduate student in a seminar with other specialists, compared the "rainbow books" published at the beginning of the war with the actual documents released afterward. The British blue books and the German white book proved to be fairly reliable, but the Austrian red book, the Russian orange book, and especially the French yellow book proved to be unreliable. The French yellow book contained alterations of dates, omissions, additions, and condensations aimed at placing *guilt* for the war upon Germany. Discoveries like these led scholars to speak of shared *responsibility.* These revisionist views caused Bernadotte E. Schmitt to put the heaviest responsibility for the war upon Germany, while Sidney B. Fay of Harvard put it upon Russia, followed by Austria and France. Russia's total mobilization, which changed a local Balkan conflict into a world war, and Austria's desire to punish Serbia (for the death of Archduke Francis Ferdinand) beyond what a sovereign nation-state would bear made them most responsible.

The same process of revisionism has taken place in the study of the causes of World War II. The first casualty of wartime hysteria is usually the truth.

American Historians

Perhaps because the people of the United States were so busy subduing their land, they were slow to develop the national consciousness that demands historical literature. In addition, until the American Revolution their past was closely twined with that of England, and history books produced there were available to Americans.

German influences have left their mark on American historical activity: the Ph.D. degree as a requirement for most teachers, the seminar as a method of instruction, the monograph as a format for reporting research, the professionalization and institutionalization of history in the universities, and the emphasis on history as a science.

America has, however, produced indigenous interpretations of history. Frederick Jackson Turner developed the geographic or frontier school of history, and Charles A. Beard and Mary R. Beard, working on the origins of the Constitution of the United States, developed what became a school of economic determinism.

American historians in each era have in some form or another introduced God into the interpretation of history. During the colonial era Puritan clergymen stated that the personal God of Calvinism was taking care of the elect nation in the wilderness. During the national era, when history was written by patricians, God was looked upon as the absolute in the fashion of Hegelian idealism. God thus conceived was the spirit behind American progress and democracy. After the Civil War, when historical writing became the work of professional historians, God was looked upon as the guarantor of evolutionary progress or as a part of that process. Such was the view of men like John Fiske.

The Colonial Era (to 1775)

Southern colonial history was regional in nature and was written mainly in Virginia. **John Smith**'s (1580–1631) pamphlet *A True Relation of Such Occurrences and Accidents of Note as Hath Happened in Virginia Since the First Planting of That Colony,* published in 1608, describes the sufferings of the early settlers in Jamestown and their relations with the Indians. Although Smith's temper and egocentricity are evident in his work, this pamphlet is generally accurate and gives one some understanding of the settlers' problems, which Smith discussed more fully in his *General History of Virginia, New England, and the Summer Isles* (1624). **William Byrd**'s (1674–1744) *History of the Dividing Line Betwixt Virginia and North Carolina* presents a faithful picture of life on the southern frontier.

Puritan historical writing in colonial New England was less spontaneous and objective, and more theological, than that in the southern colonies. The Puritans saw history as being controlled by a personal, sovereign God and as composed of deeds done by men for the glory of God. **William Bradford** (1590–1657) is in some ways the father of American history. His history *Of Plymouth Plantation* was not published even in part until about 1855, and the complete original manuscript was lost until 1896, when it was found in the library of the bishop of London. This manuscript was presented to the Massachusetts Historical Society, which published it in 1912. Bradford, who prized accuracy as much as Thucydides had, provided in this work a prime source of information for events in Plymouth from 1620 to 1646. Simply written and documented by experience as well as original written materials, it has as its main theme the providence of God in the daily life of the colony. **John Winthrop**'s (1588–1649) journal, *The History of New England from 1630 to 1649* deals with life and problems in the Boston and Salem areas, but in a more disconnected fashion.

Cotton Mather (1663–1728), who graduated from Harvard at age 15, had his *Magnalia Christi Americana* published in London in 1702. This work is a history of the church in New England from 1620 to 1698. Mather wrote it to demonstrate God's providence in the history of this colony of chosen people, so that future generations might glorify God, the enemies of the faith might be refuted, and the unrighteous might be warned. Mather began with the planting of the colonies and ended with the Salem witchcraft trials. His dislike for the Quakers and the Indians is apparent in this first "American history by an American." Mather used the word *American* for the people, and he boasted that Harvard had created more critical minds than English universities had. Other Puritan writers also emphasized the gracious favor of a personal, sovereign God toward His elect people in the wilderness.

The National or Middle Era (1776–1865)

History was written in this era by patricians who had inherited wealth or made it early enough in life to retire. Writing history was for them a hobby or avocation. During this era of romanticism, the role of God in history was still emphasized but the personal God of Calvinism became in some cases more of a theological absolute under the influence of German idealistic philosophy. God is immanent in human affairs for the "chosen Americans." A patriotic, liberal, democratic, and Protestant note entered history. History became deeds done for the chosen nation's good in its progress toward ever-increasing liberty. Parkman and Motley wrote colorful, episodic narrative history that appealed to the emotions.

If great national histories such as Bancroft's were to be written, much raw material had to be provided. Individuals like **Thomas Hutchinson** (1711–1780), author of *The History of the Colony of Massachusetts Bay* (1760–1768), provided regional or provincial local history of New England. Alexander Hewat wrote histories of South Carolina and Georgia, and Robert Proud did one of Pennsylvania. **Jeremy Belknap** (1744–1798), a graduate of Harvard and, like most historians of this era, a minister, wrote a three-volume *History of New Hampshire* (1784–1792) based on original sources. He discussed not only the geographic and natural history of the colony, but also, in two volumes, its history to 1790. This is probably the best of the histories of the separate colonies. Belknap started the *American Biographical Dictionary,* forerunner of the *Dictionary of American Biography.* He also helped to found in 1791 the Massachusetts Historical Society.

Others collected primary documents and published them, many of which were used by later synthesizers of American national history. **Peter Force** (1790–1868), a printer-journalist, was guaranteed $228,000 by the federal government to collect and edit documents dealing with the origins and development of the American colonies. Between 1837 and 1853 nine volumes of the *American Archives* were published. The holdings of the Library of Congress, particularly Thomas Jefferson's library (which had been purchased by the government), added to the mass of data available to historians.

Jared Sparks (1789–1866), a Harvard graduate and Unitarian minister in Baltimore, also collected materials. In 1827 he obtained about 20,000 of George Washington's letters and took them to Boston (later they were acquired by the Library of Congress). In addition he secured seventy volumes of Washington's manuscripts. Between 1834 and 1837 he published the twelve-volume *Writings of George Washington,* **volume 1 of which is *The Life of George Washington.*** Sparks became the McLean professor of history at Harvard in 1839, thus occupying the first chair for the teaching of history in the United States.

The publication of state histories and historical documents was followed by the writing of national histories by gifted amateurs. **George Bancroft** (1800–1891) won his A.B. at Harvard at 17 and his Ph.D. in philology in 1820 at the University of Göttingen. He returned from Germany to tutor in Greek at Harvard and to spread German culture enthusiastically in the United States. He was for a time Secretary of the Navy under President James Polk, and he founded the United States Naval Academy at Annapolis.

While on diplomatic duty in England from 1846 to 1849, Bancroft had opportunity to study materials relating to American history in the British Museum and the Public Record Office. He claimed to have spent over $100,000 in obtaining books or copies of original documents, but six thousand sets of his history were sold and earned $1,000,000. He began writing his ten-volume work, *History of the United States from the Discovery of the American Continent,* in 1823; the first volume was published in 1834 and the last in 1874.

Bancroft's regard for the American people led him to express ideas similar in form to the later concept of "manifest destiny." His faith in American nationalism and democracy with liberty for all, which he felt developed among early German tribes, resulted in Bancroft's lauding Jacksonian democracy. While not as insistent as the Puritans had been on the role of God in American affairs, he believed in a Providence that was immanent in America's history and that sponsored its progress to the winning of liberty in the revolution. While he emphasized political, military, and socioreligious history and excluded geographic and economic factors, and while he sometimes failed to quote his sources exactly, he did give an accurate description of national patriotic psychology in the first half of the nineteenth century. With Bancroft, American history "came of age."

Francis Parkman (1823–1893) wrote about the Anglo-French struggle for America and competition for the allegiance of the Indians, using a literary style characterized by vivid word pictures. He carefully collected original manuscripts, interviewed participants in events about which he wrote, and visited battlefield sites. Such books as his *History of the Conspiracy of Pontiac and the War of the North American Tribes Against the English Colonies After the Conquest of Canada* (1851) were the results of this careful study, carried on at the expense of his eyesight. He graphically described the Indian culture and forest life that he so much loved. His Protestant Anglo-Saxon bias is apparent in his contrast of free New England with absolutist, monarchical France.

Scientific History (1865–1903)

After the Civil War American historians fell under the spell of von Ranke, who insisted on reproducing history as it was, using the seminar, quoting accurately, documenting carefully, and writing monographs. The American Historical Association was founded in 1884 to help set standards and to give historians opportunity to discuss their craft in regular meetings. *The American Historical Review* was founded in 1895 as the official voice of the association. This quarterly journal consisted of learned, highly documented articles on special facets of history, bibliographical articles, unpublished documents, reviews of new books, and news of the profession.

Between 1880 and 1890 the teaching of history was institutionalized in university graduate schools. It was also professionalized as scholars with Ph.D.'s, mostly from Germany, began to do research, write books, and teach in the fields of their specialties. History was considered a science based on sources rather than a philosophic or artistic endeavor. The scientific method, exhaustive research, and alleged objectivity became trademarks of the scholarly historian. Except for Fiske's identification of God with the evolutionary process, the divine element was minimized in history.

Henry Brooks Adams (1838–1918), professor of medieval history at Harvard, began to use the seminar method in 1872. He trained many fine historians, such as H. O. Taylor, who specialized in medieval intellectual history, and Edward Channing, who concentrated on American history. Students today might find Adams's examinations irksome because he asked questions to which he said he had no answer. In his nine-volume *History of the United States of America* published between 1889 and 1891, he developed the idea that history might be an exact science that will yield an all-embracing evolutionary law of history. He finally renounced this idea and turned to the Roman Catholic church for the authority he had not found in history. Like Bancroft he emphasized the heritage of Anglo-Saxon life in the development of the United States. Hermann von Holst and James Schouler also produced histories of the United States in this period.

John Fiske (1842–1901), Harvard-educated popularizer of history in lectures and books, wrote the two-volume *Discovery of America, with Some Account of Ancient America and the Spanish Conquest* (1892). In it he revealed his interest in Spencerian evolution in American history. This evolution would guarantee progress of the middle-class, Protestant civilization under a federal democracy. He laid most stress on aboriginal America and its discovery. Unfortunately he failed to do the needed critical research because he was interested in popularization.

John Bach McMaster (1852–1932) was a civil engineer who in 1883 was made professor of history at the University of Pennsylvania. Between 1883 and 1913 he published the eight-volume *History of the People of the United States, from the Revolution to the Civil War.* The word *people* in the title indicates a new direction in historical writing—an emphasis on the common man, who through education will make democratic progress. McMaster turned to newspaper files of the past to gain an understanding of the ordinary person, and thus he pioneered in the use of newspaper serials as a documentary source for social history. He was also one of the first to see the importance of the West in American history.

George Louis Beer (1872–1920) was perhaps the foremost writer of a group that began to study British colonial history as a broader background for the American Revolution. His books *British Colonial Policy, 1754–1765* (1907), *The Origins of the British Colonial System, 1578–1660*

(1908), and *The Old Colonial System, 1660–1754* (1912) set forth the British policy toward the thirteen colonies and the colonies' fear of France, which until 1763 bound them to England. He did not stress the failures of George III in governing the colonies. **Charles M. Andrews** (1863–1943) and later **Lawrence Henry Gipson** (1880–1971), author of the fifteen-volume *British Empire Before the American Revolution: Provincial Characteristics and Sectional Tendencies in the Era Preceding the American Crisis* (1936–1970), continued in a scholarly, well-documented fashion the approach pioneered by Beer.

Vernon Louis Parrington (1871–1929) pointed out in *Main Currents in American Thought: An Interpretation of American Literature from the Beginnings to 1920* (1927–1930) that literature reflects the history of the day and in turn that ideals in literature influence historical writing. Although unsympathetic with the Puritans, he did show the importance of ideas in historical development. **Merle E. Curti** (1897–) in *The Growth of American Thought* (1943) showed the relation between ideas and American history more objectively. **Frederick Jackson Turner** (1861–1932), professor for years at the University of Wisconsin, reacted against the emphasis on Anglo-Saxon institutions and ideals in previous histories of America and used instead geography or the frontier as the key to unlock the story of American development. Turner, Curti, and Parrington thus helped pioneer new, indigenous approaches to history. Turner's emphasis on the Western frontier had been prefigured by **Theodore Roosevelt** (1858–1919) in his six-volume work, *The Winning of the West: An Account of the Exploration and Settlement of Our Country from the Alleghanies to the Pacific* (1889–1896). **Herbert E. Bolton** (1870–1953) used the frontier theme to explain the development of Latin American history.

A later development is multivolume treatments of American history in which a specialist writes each volume under the leadership of a general editor. Albert Bushnell Hart's 28-volume *The American Nation: A History from Original Sources by Associated Scholars* (1904–1918), Allen Johnson's 50-volume Chronicles of America series (1919–1921), and the 13-volume History of American Life series (1927–1952) are good examples. The endless production of Ph.D. dissertations continues to provide more material for later syntheses.

Relativistic History (1903–)

During the twentieth century many European historians rebelled against the Rankean cult of objectively reconstructed political history. A similar rebellion occurred after World War I in America, where scientific history had been promoted by such men as E. P. Cheyney, who insisted that there are "laws" of history. The rebels favored a presentist approach and denied the possibility of scientific objectivity to the point that, according to Benedetto Croce, history is only contemporary thought upon the past. James Harvey Robinson (1863–1936) and later Carl L. Becker (1873–1945) were in the vanguard of the New School. They approached history in a relativistic-idealistic way, using the scientific method in the study of documents, but insisting that the subjective element be recognized in their interpretation. Historians today seem to be moving in the direction of an intelligent synthesis of these two outlooks.

While this survey of the major historians has been brief, it has included what might be called the classical writers who best illustrate each era. It also reveals the influence of the prevailing climate of opinion on the writing of history. Both Christian and secular historians have usually sought to obtain the best sources of information and write history in as unbiased a fashion as human beings can, influenced as they are by their times.

Annotated Bibliography

The Poetry of History (1947) by Emery E. Neff and *The Art of History* (1965) by John B. Black both treated historians of the eighteenth-century Enlightenment in some detail. George P. Gooch in *History and Historians in the Nineteenth Century* (1952) ably discussed such writers as von Ranke. *Some Historians of Modern Europe* (1942), edited by Bernadotte E. Schmitt, covers much of the same ground. A helpful survey of English historians is available in *The Evolution of British Historiography* (1964) edited by John R. Hale.

Critical evaluations of the life and writings of the main American historians can be found in Michael Kraus's *The Writing of American History* (1953). *The American Historian* (1960) by Harvey Wish, *American History and American Historians* (1952) by Hugh H. Bellot, and *The Marcus W. Jernegan Essays in*

American Historiography (1937) edited by William T. Hutchinson all give additional data on important American historians and their works. John Higham's many writings in this field will also be helpful.

American Themes (1968), edited by Frank Otto Gatell and Allen Weinstein, will be helpful in studying the various approaches to American history. *The Reconstruction of American History* (1962) edited by John Higham is another helpful survey of these approaches. *American History* (1971) edited by George A. Billias and Gerald N. Grob and *Historical Interpretations and American Historianship* (1966) by Jennings B. Sanders both have helpful sections on the interpretation of American history.

Writers such as George Bancroft, John L. Motley, Francis Parkman, William H. Prescott, Peter Force, Jeremy Belknap, and Jared Sparks are discussed in helpful chapters in either *History as Romantic Art* (1959) by David Levin or *The Middle Group of American Historians* (1917) by John Spencer Bassett. Specialized works are available for the historiography of other countries and regions.

CHAPTER 5

Schools of Historical Interpretation

After making careful inquiry into the genuineness, integrity, and credibility of his information and after making valid inductions or inferences from his data, the historian must begin integrating the data. What meaning can he assign to it, or what interpretation will he follow? Is meaning to be found only in the historical process, as Karl Marx insisted, or is there a revelational ultimate to which all must be related, as the Christian historian insists? Are there patterns in history? Is a historian a philosopher, either implicitly or explicitly? In all of this, deductions must be based on data and inductions. Patterns must correspond to the data and be coherent, cogent, and comprehensible to the reader.

In classifying his data the historian must distinguish between the immediate, secondary, or contingent cause of a historical happening and the mediate, remote, or final causes behind the event. Martin Luther's posting of the Ninety-five Theses on the church door on 31 October 1517 was the contingent cause or occasion for the coming of the Reformation. The assassination of the Archduke Francis Ferdinand, heir to the Austrian throne, by Gavrilo Princip at Serajevo in June 1914 was the spark that set off World War I. Behind that incident, however, were such major causes as imperial tensions, economic rivalries, and competing sets of alliances. Historical events may have a single secondary cause, but the remote or final causes are complex and multiple.

The historian's own world and life view and his values will be important factors in his search for ultimate causation, something that every historian does either implicitly or explicitly. His own biases as well as those of the age will affect his outlook. His total view of life—whether atheistic like Marx's, idealistic like Georg Hegel's, or theistic like Augustine's—will influence him in assigning ultimate meaning to his data. The school or philosophy of history to which he belongs also affects his interpretation of the material. If he is an economic determinist, he will elevate economics to the level of a final cause. His view of life as well as his view of history will affect his interpretation.

During the last half of the nineteenth century, questions of causation, whether secondary or final, did not arise because historians like Leopold von Ranke, John B. Bury, Henry T. Buckle, and Henry Brooks Adams believed that use of the scientific method leads one to general laws of history that are valid inductions from the facts. These historians believed they were not importing these laws into history but deriving them from it. Crane Brinton thought his studies had uncovered a generally applicable law of revolutions.

In the twentieth century such neoidealists as Wilhelm Dilthey, while interested in critical philosophy which involves historical epistemology, thought that the historian could only "relive" the past subjectively. Benedetto Croce and Robin G. Collingwood, though they both used the scientific method in checking their sources, argued that history is a subjective affair at the point of interpretation. The later, closely related relativists, such as Charles A. Beard and Carl L. Becker, though they also used the scientific method in gathering information, also argued that the interpretation of data is subjective because of the interpreter's biases and his climate of opinion. This approach seems to be more congenial to contemporary historians than that of the scientific school.

The historian's record of the past has two elements. The first is the facts or information without which one can know nothing about these initially objective and valid happenings.

This information comes in the form of testimony or records, whether documentary or archaeological. Except in the case of archaeology one can know events only indirectly through the individuals whose testimony or records have survived, and these persons may have been limited by their physical proximity to the event, their ability to report adequately, and their biases. The second element in the writing of history is the interpreter of history himself. His data may be incomplete, forged, or biased. He must determine which of his material is significant and which is not. Unlike the scientist the historian is not impersonal with respect to his data; he is a part of it. He has to take into account his own personal and environmental biases. Both the witness of the event and the later interpreter, then, must be reckoned with in the writing of history. Are we shut up to agnosticism about the past or relativistic contemporary thought upon the past, or are there some things that can be known?

The happenings in history and the information in documents and in archaeological objects of the past are outside the historian's mind. Through scientific study of his artifacts and documents, the historian can come to know the objective incident to a great extent. He can be reasonably certain concerning an event when at least two independent witnesses agree on the facts in their records, and when fellow historians, often hostile to his interpretation, verify his data independently and come to the same conclusion about the facts. There is a surprising amount of consensus among historians on the basic facts and on many conclusions about the past. If a historian's findings are consistent with his documents and coherent and cogent as well, they provide a logic that will commend them to the profession.

Because history is complex and multiple in causation, the problem of the why of history, of its meaning or interpretation, is not easy. The discussion can begin with a modified form of a statement by H. Stuart Hughes in "The Historian and the Social Scientist" (1963):[1] the levels of interpretation are semantic interpretations, statements, schemes, and speculation in a broadening vista of generalization from narrower to broader levels of integration.

1. "The Historian and the Social Scientist," in *Generalizations in Historical Writing,* ed. Alexander V. Riasanovsky and Barnes Riznik (Philadelphia: University of Pennsylvania, 1963), pp. 18–59.

Meaning of happenings in the past will at times be logically arranged around **semantic interpretations,** words that have an integrative or synthetic function. Anyone working with documents from such eighteenth-century intellectual leaders as Montesquieu, Voltaire, or Jean Jacques Rousseau soon concludes that the words *perfectibility* and *progress* describe their world and life view; *science* and *scientific method* express their method for progressing to perfection. The words *faith* and the *priesthood of believers* give meaning to documents from Luther and his friends in the sixteenth century. *Liberalism* well describes the desire of nineteenth-century thinkers for political, economic, religious, and intellectual freedom for the individual. The word *revolution* integrates the data made available by studies of forcible social change.

Statements or concepts form broader generalizations than semantic interpretations. These statements are in many cases valid inductions from the material produced by research. The writer found in studying nineteenth-century missions in Africa that missionaries such as David Livingstone, who served in East and Central Africa, and George Grenfell, who served in the Congo region, were the first to map the outlines of Africa's great river systems. They were able pioneer explorers, later honored for their work by the Royal Geographical Society of England. That missionaries in Africa were the leading explorers is a statement that grows out of the evidence, an induction, not one that the interpreter imports into the evidence. A number of missionaries imported plants to provide new cash crops for the indigenous population. Missionaries built the earliest elementary and secondary educational institutions and opened industrial schools long before the imperial powers in charge did anything. Robert Moffat in South Africa and George L. Pilkington in Uganda reduced native languages to written form. Defeat in war usually strengthens the opposition and weakens the government. In conquest the higher culture, even though its carriers have been physically conquered, absorbs the lower culture. These illustrate the way in which statements may be validly induced from the data and readily checked by others. Historians have made few generalizations on this level.

The third level of generalization can be called **scheme.** Material from research is synthesized to the point where uniformities or regularities seem to emerge from the data. Some go so far as to call these generalizations "laws" of history. Brinton pointed out that revolutions move steadily to the left: the earlier left puts its program into effect and is then forced to a more moderate position by a new left with an even more radical program. This alternation continues until a group gains enough power to stop the revolution or until the public, psychologically exhausted by change and violence, turns to moderates and opposes the radicals. Brinton believed this "law" of revolution to be a valid induction from the revolutions he had studied. E. P. Cheyney believed that he too had identified several laws in history.

The ubiquity and universality of sin in human history led neo-orthodox thinkers to conclude that there are valid principles or statements of historical fact. Some think Richard M. Nixon's fall after Watergate and Germany's fall and division after World War II illustrate moral law in history. The transformation of persons and nations that have professed Christianity is used by some historians to point up the principle of the transforming power of Christianity.

The fourth level of generalization involves what one might call **speculation** or metahistory. While critical philosophy studies how man knows what he knows in any field, speculative philosophy concerns itself with the grand picture, the relation of the part to the whole, or the relation of the data to an ultimate factor or Person. This level of generalization is associated with philosophies of history whereas the level of schematization is more properly linked with schools of history. These schools often raise such secondary, contingent causes as the economic, geographic, or personal to the level of final interpretation.

The ideas of Augustine, Marx, Hegel, Oswald Spengler and Arnold J. Toynbee all fit into the category of speculative history. These men linked their semantic concepts, statements, or schemes of history with an ultimate pattern of meaning. Such explanations are holistic. The Christian interpreter of history, who uses the scientific method to gather data and make inductions, introduces the data of revelation in an attempt to create an ultimate philosophy that embraces all the evidence.

The influence of von Ranke caused scientific and even relativistic historians to shy away from this approach, accusing it of theologizing or philosophizing beyond what the material warrants. It should be clearly understood, however, that whether one holds to a school or philosophy of history, he has in the first case an implicit, and in the second an explicit, interpretation of history. Philosophy or revelation denied entrance by the front door will creep in the back. Marxists can be as dogmatic as the theologians they ridicule. No one can escape having a philosophy of history if he thinks at all seriously about the human past. It may be implicit and he may not recognize it, but it is there. Honest historians have to recognize that they integrate history for meaning on all four levels described thus far.

Use of the terms *school of history* and *philosophy of history* leads to the question of how they differ. Allan Nevins in chapter 9 of *The Gateway to History* gave more attention to this distinction than have other historians. Generally those with positivistic tendencies gravitate to a school of history; and those who recognize the problems of relativism, to a philosophy of history. Proponents of schools of history are more often time- and space-oriented and use horizontal, temporal, and earthly factors, such as man or nature, to explain history. Philosophers of history, on the other hand, seek ultimate meaning beyond as well as in history. They introduce vertical, timeless or eternal, and spiritual forces, such as God or an absolute, to find meaning in history. Schools are more concerned with relative factors; philosophies with absolutes that include all historical data in a comprehensive whole. Secondary, contingent, or immedate causes are emphasized by schools of historical interpretation; primary causation by philosophies. Schools seem to stress the part, philosophies the whole. Schools are primarily concerned with what they hope are objective inductions; philosophies with general and ultimate meaning in the historical process or beyond, seeking by reflection to formulate a holistic view of history.

Because schools of interpretation raise one factor to the level of a final explanation, they often have an implicit and unrecognized philosophy of history. Thus the difference between the two is not so much one of essence as of degree and scope. Schools tend to oversimplify by making one factor, such as geography or economics, the final one while forgetting the complexity of human history. They tend to confuse data and meaning and to ignore final truth of any kind. The Beards, who originated the economic interpretation of the American Constitution, and Frederick Jackson Turner, who developed the frontier theory of American history, even though seeking explanations on the temporal level, tended to raise their interpretations to the level of ultimate or final meaning. This contradicted their claims to being purely scientific in their approach to and explanation of historical data. Schools reject ultimate or final truth in favor of partial explanations. Whether one adheres to a school of history or a philosophy of history—and all hold to one or the other at least implicitly—one should get the story straight by careful, honest, and impartial development of evidence from documents. The interpreter should be as aware as possible of his own psychological bent and that of his times, and he should seek to keep these in control as he handles the evidence. If this were always done, there would be fewer schools and philosophies of history.

History is **didactic,** teaching men to become either wiser or better, according to most ancient and medieval historians. While not strictly a school of historical interpretation, this approach has been a dominant motif in historiography at times. Polybius believed that men would be wiser leaders if they read his history. Plutarch, Tacitus, Livy, Bede, and Gregory of Tours all believed that history offers examples of moral and immoral lives and that men will follow the good they see in history. Tacitus thought that the desire to be highly regarded by posterity makes men seek the good and shun the bad. Montaigne thought that the moral lessons to be drawn from history constitute its main value. Lord Bolingbroke in the eighteenth century thought that history is philosophy teaching by example. With the advent of the scientific approach to history, scholars disdained this approach and thought that one should study history for the satisfaction of curiosity rather than for utilitarian purposes. Perhaps more attention to this didactic approach would get the general public to read history once again.

James A. Froude, von Ranke, Jules Michelet, and James F. Rhodes leaned to the idea that history is **political,** the story of how men have governed themselves. History becomes the study of past politics and politics becomes present history. This view, along with the "drum and battle" theory (that history is the story of what great military leaders have done), has decidedly fallen out of favor. One has to recognize, however, that certain battles have had a great impact on history. The battle of the Plains of Abraham between the French and English ended French rule in North America and left the American colonists feeling secure enough to revolt against British mercantilism. Saratoga was a decisive battle in the American Revolution because it raised colonial morale and brought France and Spain into the war on the Colonies' side.

The **sociological** school of historical interpretation began with Auguste Comte (1798–1857), who insisted that there are laws in history that can be used for social engineering. Environmental factors are more important in history than hereditary ones. Comte set forth his system in his *Course of Positive Philosophy* (1830–1842).

Society, according to Comte, is more important than the individual and might even be an organic entity. Historians can discover laws of social change that are universally valid and that can be used to direct the development of society. Use of the scientific method on social data will result in the induction of these laws. He thought that up to the year 1350, men had been under the influence of myths, theological explanations of the universe. After that, man was governed by metaphysical laws of philosophy. In 1789 man entered the positive period during which social laws, derived from empirical study of social phenomena, became the basis for a new humanity. These laws of social science would be as valid as those of natural science and could be used in human development. Sociology, of which Comte was the founder, would result in the creation of social laws that could be used to predict and control social change. Comte did not follow his own idea of scientific social law faithfully, however, when he formulated an unscientific religion of humanity, complete with creed and liturgy.

One might say that the communists' attempt to modify man by changing his environment is an application of Comte's idea. Science can be used to modify environment, but human nature is not so easily controlled. For that reason one who would change must resort to force and make men obey because of fear. Western sociology today simply describes social phenomena that may be helpful in social change. It more modestly refuses to elevate its findings to universally valid laws.

The **biographical** or "great man" school of history may be an extension of man's desire to worship. When man ceases to believe in and worship a transcendent figure, he turns for an object of reverence to man himself. Thomas Carlyle's

(1795–1881) eulogies of Frederick the Great and Oliver Cromwell are more characteristic of the earlier biographical school than the later one. Lytton Strachey (1880–1932) in his *Eminent Victorians* (1918)[2] and *Queen Victoria* (1921) tended to debunk his subjects, showing their weaknesses and foibles more than their good points. Stefan Zweig (1881–1942), borrowing from Sigmund Freud, resorted to psychoanalysis in dealing with the abnormal in his subjects. Zweig suggested in *Marie Antoinette: The Portrait of an Average Woman* (1932) that the French Revolution might never have occurred if Louis XVI and Marie Antoinette had been able to adjust sexually through a minor operation. Erik H. Erikson (1902–) in *Young Man Luther: A Study in Psychoanalysis and History* (1962) has continued this biographical, psychoanalytical approach. This may be a helpful technique, but it must be used with great care. Not enough data is available for other than tentative judgments concerning a deceased individual.

Carlyle declared on the first page of his *On Heroes, Hero-Worship, and the Heroic in History* (1841) that history is "at bottom the history of the great men who have worked here." Men are, to borrow Sidney Hooks's phrase, "event-making" rather than merely stepping into an environment or situation that is conducive to their having an impact upon history. They mold history by intellect and character rather than affecting it by arising out of favorable circumstances. What Carlyle failed to remember, however, is that even great men are as much creatures as creators of their times.

Good biography should be based on a patient, careful study of the sources and should recreate, in as unbiased a manner as possible, the subject's times, his life and work, and his impact on his day. Biography thereby humanizes the past. It can also have moral value as the reader sees the good and bad results of the subject's character and his courses of action. The great-man theory of history erred in putting heredity above environment.

The **economic** school of history, which has won many adherents over the years, is not identical with Marxism. This school does not buy the Marxist philosophy of history, which is based on the concept that matter in motion is the basic stuff of history. It does borrow the Marxist tenet, however, that

2. Strachey's "eminent Victorians" were Cardinal Manning, Florence Nightingale, Matthew Arnold, and General Charles Gordon.

the economic factor is the most important one in human affairs. Both Paul in I Thessalonians 4:11–12 and Christ during His temptation (see Matt. 4) admitted the significance of the economic motive, but they did not see it as determining history. Men act from several motives, not from one.

Charles A. Beard (1874–1948) in *An Economic Interpretation of the Constitution of the United States* (1913) claimed that the founding fathers, whose investments in land and bonds were considerable, created a strong federal system out of a desire to protect these investments. Beard did not claim, however, that all American history must be explained in economic terms. Max Weber (1864–1920) in *The Protestant Ethic and the Spirit of Capitalism* (1904–1905) and R. H. Tawney tried to account for the Reformation by seeing it as an economic phenomenon that helped create the modern capitalistic system. Calvinism's emphasis on thrift, allowance for usury, simple life style, and doctrine of vocation (i.e., the call of God to a vocation) may well have stimulated capitalism, but this is different from saying that religion created capitalism, which in one form or another has existed since ancient times. Lewis B. Namier studied the financial status of members of Parliament in 1761 in an effort to determine the extent to which economics had affected political life in that era. He published the fruit of his research in a two-volume work, *The Structure of Politics at the Accession of George III* (1929).

These interpreters have performed a useful service by insisting that the historian take into account how men made a living in the era under study, for economics is a contingent, secondary, conditioning factor in human action. Such interpreters err if they make economics the final, determinative factor, because in the complicated structure that is history as event, men do not always know what their economic interest is. They want to have more money to spend, for example, but they often fail to realize that inflation, which is epidemic in modern governmental structures and which wrecks an economy, only gives them the illusion of having more money. While they receive more dollars every year, they are able to buy less and less for each dollar. Economic determinism also ignores man's free will. While economic influence is apparent in history, economic determinism is not. Secondary causes in history may include goods and services, but they also include other factors.

The **geographic** or frontier school of history, which is associated with the name of Frederick Jackson Turner (1861–1932), emphasizes the environmental, geographic factor almost to the exclusion of other factors. Turner, who had been born on the Wisconsin frontier, where the Indian fur-trade thrived, reacted against the "germ" theory of the origins of American institutions. This theory, taught by Henry Brooks Adams in the graduate seminar at Johns Hopkins University, traced democracy to the ancient Germans, who developed it in their tribal assemblies. It is true that they developed local, participatory democracy, but British institutions had more influence in the development of American democracy. Others before Turner had similarly emphasized the role of geography in human history. Montesquieu in *The Spirit of Laws* (1748) held that geography helps determine a people's sociological outlook, which in turn influences the form of government they adopt. Henry T. Buckle (1821–1862) gave geography an important place in the two-volume *History of Civilization in England* (1857–1861). Ellsworth Huntington (1876–1947), and later Ellen Churchill Semple (1863–1932) in *American History and Its Geographic Conditions* (1903), continued this emphasis. Walter P. Webb (1888–1963) applied the same principle to developments on the great plains of America and later to world history.

Turner, following a clue from the Italian economist Achille Loria, carefully studied governmental census reports of the frontier. He concluded from his statistics, charts, and graphs, as well as from his own experience, that "the existence of an area of free land, its continuous recession, and the advance of American settlement westward" was of prime importance in explaining the history of America. The needs of the frontier developed individualism, self-governing institutions, thrift, cooperation, and a sense of national welfare that offset sectionalism. He first enunciated this theory in his paper "The Significance of the Frontier in American History," which he read on 12 July 1893 to members of the American Historical Association, meeting in Chicago during the World Fair.

Turner forgot or ignored the fact that bicameral government, widely used on the state level in the West, had come with the settlers from the East, and before that it had been imported from England. He also forgot that after the Civil War people had to pay for land on the frontier and that land companies frequently exploited the land. Thus instead of being free and a safety valve from failure in Eastern cities, land was relatively expensive. After the Civil War there was almost as much migration to the factories in the cities as to land on the frontier.

Despite these criticisms, geography is important in historical study. The frontier concept helps one understand the influence of geography on human development. It is interesting that all the great religions rose in arid or semiarid areas in Asia. Man is, however, the dynamic factor and can adapt or rise above static geography through technology. Thus Americans can live comfortably even on the DEW line in Greenland.

James Harvey Robinson (1863–1936), James T. Shotwell, Preserved Smith, and Carl L. Becker have been associated with what has been called the New School or **synthetic** school of history. These men used scientific methods to discover, evaluate, and present the many factors that create a particular group approach to life. They wanted to reconstruct the whole past rather than study only one important factor. They put understanding above causation. In addition to being positivistic in their approach, they usually employed biological and social evolution in their attempt to understand history. They did admit the need to consider the many factors that operate in history, but their presuppositions often led them to merely naturalistic explanations that ignored ideals and religion. They allied themselves with other social scientists by insisting that history should contribute to social reform in the present. Schools of interpretation have focused attention on often-neglected factors in history, and in doing so they have performed a valuable service. But too often they have tended to raise their key interpretive concepts to the level of relative absolutes. They have not always understood that their supposedly empirical economic, geographic, or biographical views have underlying naturalistic philosophies. They have forgotten that on the secondary, contingent level, causation is multiple and complex. They have ignored the complexity and plurality of human motivation and ruled out God or other ultimates. They have confused secondary, contingent factors with primary causes. Their answers have all been on the horizontal level in the temporal process of history, centered on man, nature, or process. They have left little room for any divine element in history.

Annotated Bibliography

Gordon H. Clark in *Historiography, Secular and Religious* (1971) critically discussed various schools and philosophies of history from a biblical, theistic viewpoint. Allan Nevins in *The Gateway to History* (1963) has the most helpful survey of the various schools of history (pp. 265–71 and elsewhere). Books mentioned in this chapter also help present the views of particular schools of history. James Harvey Robinson in *The New History* (1912) ably summarized the concepts of the New School. Several historians in *The Interpretation of History* (1943), edited by Joseph R. Strayer, discussed several of the schools mentioned in this chapter.

CHAPTER 6

Philosophies of History: Pessimistic and Optimistic

Although Voltaire did not himself develop a full-fledged philosophy of history, John B. Bury credited him with coining the phrase "philosophy of history" as early as 1756. It must be emphasized that even those who hold to a school of interpretation have an underlying philosophy of history, though they may not recognize it because it is implicit rather than explicit. Each interpreter approaches his material with some world and life view that he either recognizes and honestly tries to relate to the data or that he does not recognize in his preoccupation with the scientific side of historical study. History demands an answer to the why as well as to the who or what, when, and where of the data. Reflection or speculation has to follow investigation. One moves from the incident to information about it, to inquiry concerning that information, to inductions from the data, and finally to interpretation that relates the parts to the whole. Rational beings have an urge to correlate data.

A philosophy of history is an attempt to interpret systematically the historical process by a principle that unifies the results of research and points to an ultimate meaning behind the process. It involves systematic reflection on scientifically derived data about the past. All the parts are unified to form a whole with ultimate meaning. The philosophic idea is not usually derived from the data but is brought to it from the outside and related to it. This idea may be matter in motion, as it was for Karl Marx; the absolute, as for Georg Hegel; or God, as for Christian historians. Much of the critical philosophy that deals with the problem of epistemology in historical research has been done by philosophers, but the speculative philosophy that unifies data and relates it to an ultimate has been done by both philosophers and historians.

The first attempts at a philosophy of history had to wait for the development of the Hebrew-Christian ideas that time is linear and that God intervenes in history. The Greeks saw the world as static, operating in endless cycles. They made no provision for any kind of progress. The Jewish-Christian outlook required that data must ultimately be related to revelation in the Bible as well as to nature and history. Thus Christians were the first to develop a full-scale philosophy of history.

Most modern historians, being positivists or relativists, will have nothing to do with philosophy of history. Unfortunately many evangelicals have taken a similar stance, though for different reasons. Some feel that biblical prophecy provides a clear blueprint for the future, rendering history unnecessary. Others are reacting against Liberalism and the Social Gospel. The cataclysmic nature of current events, however, is creating an end-of-the-age feeling that is more compatible with historical philosophizing. Many historians are speaking out in favor of developing a philosophy of history, which they hope will help make sense of the data of historical research. One has to guard against monocausation and "presentitis" in the attempt to unify data and find some ultimate frame of reference. Here the Christian historian has a real opportunity to link information about the past with divine revelation.

Change in history must be linked with continuity. The Greeks and Oswald Spengler were impressed with change in history, while modern evolutionary historians have emphasized the element of continuity. Both must be considered. Change in history can be linked with the continuing God of revelation.

Various approaches have been used to organize philosophies of history. One is to divide them into the two categories of cyclic and linear. The Greeks, seeing the recurrence of the astronomical year, thought of time as cyclic. As pessimistic interpreters, they and Spengler linked change and continuity in history with the concept of recurring cycles. The Indians tended to follow this pattern also, but they had little interest in historical philosophizing because they considered time and present being to be illusory. The Israelites and other interpreters (who are either pessimistic-optimistic or just optimistic) have thought of time as linear, continuous, and irreversible. But the categories of cyclic and linear are not broad enough to include all philosophies.

Some use the categories of naturalistic, humanistic, and idealistic, the crux being whether nature, man, or an absolute is looked upon as the ultimate cause. But many, including most liberals, try to link man with an absolute in their interpretation. Others look upon degeneration, progress, or providence as proper categories, but in many cases historians have linked progress and providence. Some think prideful man, frustrated man, or redeemed man provide suitable frames. Others speak of physical, metaphysical, and theological approaches; Marx interpreted history from below, Hegel from within, and Augustine from above.

But the most all-inclusive categories for organizing philosophies of history are pessimistic, optimistic, and pessimistic-optimistic. The first may be symbolized by an animal exercising on a treadmill or a swinging pendulum; the second by an escalator, an incoming tide, a spiral, or an ascending graph line. The third view speaks of tension between good and evil, then a titanic clash between them, and finally the triumph of the good. This threefold organization encompasses all philosophies of history in providing broad patterns.

Pessimistic Philosophies

Pessimistic approaches to history have generally been concerned with the idea of recurrence or change in history, recurrent movement in fixed cycles. Such views usually appear in an era of crisis. Spengler developed this type of theory in Germany during the chaos at the end of World War I. Grace E. Cairns in her *Philosophies of History* traces and develops most of these approaches to historical interpretation. Such ideas seem to be based on man's understanding of the astronomical, solar, and lunar cycles. The recurrence he saw in nature he applied by analogy to human history. History, then, repeats itself continuously.

The ephemeral nature of man, of his life and work, led in the Far East to the view that the past is largely irrelevant. Taoists sought to retreat from the present and history by returning to and immersing themselves in nature. Hindus and Buddhists attempted to free themselves from material illusion by becoming absorbed ultimately into the force behind the universe. For this reason major philosophies of history have not been developed in the Far East.

Egyptians, Sumerians, Jains, Taoists, Mayans, Aztecs, and Greeks thought of history in terms of cosmic cycles. Hesiod in his *Works and Days* pictured history as a degenerative cycle. Gold, silver, bronze, and iron ages follow each other in descending value, after which the cycle is repeated. In the *Laws* and *Timaeus* Plato depicted history as a recurring cycle, governed by the hand of fate, that begins with a golden age, then witnesses its deterioration and finally its destruction.[1] Aristotle's study of nature led him to see the cyclical also and to conclude that the coming-to-be of everything is circular.[2]

Others discerned recurrent culture cycles. Ibn-Khaldun in his *Muqqadimah* (1377) posited cycles in which virile groups conquer more advanced peoples, become sedentary, and eventually succumb to invaders who are more primitive. In his book on philosophy of history, Giovanni Battista Vico spoke of recurring cultural cycles, with inner cycles of God, man, and heroes in each broad cycle. He did, however, believe that Providence invisibly guides the process to a final end that is good. Spengler, writing at the end of World War I, thought civilizations go through cycle after cycle of birth, growth, and death. Arnold J. Toynbee spoke of nondeterministic cultural cycles that can carry progress. In this he disagreed with Spengler, who saw in his cycles only degeneration. Most cyclical views, like Spengler's, have been pessimistic. The author of Ecclesiastes was impressed with cyclical determinism in nature, but he raised human history above

1. *Laws,* 3:676–78; *Timaeus,* 21–23 (91d–92c).

2. *Degeneratione et Corruptione,* 1–9, 11, 15–16 (337a, 338a).

these natural cycles by putting it under the control of God (1:1–11).

Cyclical philosophies of history are usually linked with the idea of degeneration in human affairs from a past golden age to increasingly inferior succeeding ages, until the whole process starts over again. These changes are deterministic. Nothing that man can do will alter the pattern. Needless to say, such views leave no room for any divine role in history. History is a treadmill. With one exception these pessimistic views have not appealed much to modern man, who seeks to achieve Utopia in history. The exception is the philosophy of history espoused by Spengler.

Oswald Spengler (1880–1936) studied mathematics, science, art, and history at the universities of Halle, Munich, and Berlin. He won his doctorate at the University of Berlin with a dissertation on Heraclitus, the naturalistic Greek philosopher. He taught mathematics and later history in high school, but most of his time during World War I was devoted to working in an unheated room in Munich on *The Decline of the West.* He was exempted from military service because of a bad heart. This claustrophobic, bald bachelor, who lived mostly on tea, finally completed his two-volume work, which won him fame and fortune with its end-of-the-age appeal to the disillusioned, defeated Germans. Fifty thousand copies of the first volume sold quickly after its publication in 1918. He was able to move into more luxurious and spacious quarters, which relieved his claustrophobia. The second volume of what he said was "a German philosophy" and "the philosophy of our time"[3] came out in 1922. His philosophy was pessimistic, relativistic, and deterministic.

Spengler called the basic unit in his system by the name *culture,*[4] which in each case lasted about one thousand years.[5] Each unit or organism was self-contained,[6] having no relation to other units in his system. There was no real place in his thinking for either race or nation. Each cultural cycle is a closed, organismic unit.[7] He used the analogy of spring, summer, fall, and winter to provide a morphology for his culture cycles.[8] He also used the analogy of birth, childhood,

3. *The Decline of the West,* trans. Charles Francis Atkinson, 2 vols. (New York: Knopf, 1926–1928), 1:xiv–xv.

4. Ibid., 1:21.

5. Ibid., 1:104.

6. Ibid.

7. Ibid., 1:180.

8. Ibid., vol. 1, table 1.

manhood, and old age to describe the process in the cycles.[9] He mentioned eight cultures in all, treated only six factually, and discussed the classical and Western cultures in detail.

Cultures develop from a primitive, "cultureless," "historyless" period in which the rural peasant is the key figure. A culture develops in time and as it nears its end becomes a civilization. The civilization[10] is marked by a money economy[11] and the development of an urban democracy in a megalopolis.[12] This leads to a state of war and an era of world dictatorship. The civilization ends with a clash that is followed by another "historyless" period, out of which a new culture emerges that goes through the same cycle.[13]

Each culture goes through this determined, degenerative process that is a part of the cyclical historical pattern.[14] The cycle is dominated by either blind fate or destiny in somewhat the same way that nature is bound by the law of causality.[15] Man cannot guide or change his destiny but must placidly accept it. History has no goal and exhibits no linear progress. History has "no meaning whatsoever,"[16] being characterized by sublime "purposelessness." There is no transfer from one culture to another. Each is a self-contained unit in which continuity is sacrificed to the recurrence of eternal change. Western culture entered its period of civilization about 1789[17] and neared its end during World War I. The future would be dominated by Negroid or Mongoloid people. War is the only creative force in history.[18] Truth[19] and morals[20] are relative. There is no absolute or divine in Spengler's system.

Civilizations or cultures are not the evolutionary organism of Spengler's view. They are the result of individuals reacting to each other in an aggregated society. Vitality is related to the individual rather than the civilization. Spengler forgot that civilizations borrow from one another by cultural diffusion and that much of the past lives on in the present. For example, today's basic forms of literature and patterns of philosophy are derived from the Greeks. Spengler also forgot

9. Ibid., 1:107 and table 1.

10. Ibid., 1:31.

11. Ibid., 2:96–98.

12. Ibid., 2:90.

13. Ibid., 2:464–65, 506–7.

14. Ibid., 1:21–22, 106, 109–10.

15. Ibid., 1:8, 109–10; 2:507.

16. Ibid., 2:44.

17. Ibid., 1:44–45; 2:415–16.

18. Ibid., 2:363, 440, 464–67, 507.

19. Ibid., 1:xiii, 23, 25, 46.

20. Ibid., 1:315.

that love has been as important a factor in history as has been force or hate. The buoyant and activistic outlook of Americans has made Spengler's cyclical determinism distasteful to them. History directed neither by human will nor by divine plan has no value to the modern, optimistic American outlook. Perhaps Americans need Spengler's reminder that Western civilization is declining and that its continued existence may be threatened.

Optimistic Philosophies

While pessimistic interpreters despair too much of man in history and see too little meaning in it, many optimistic interpreters expect too much from man in history and become utopian millenarians. Their romantic optimism, with its expectation of salvation in history, helps them create a "religion" of progress in irreversible time. In extreme cases their desire to make men into angels in history leads them to treat men as brutes who should be controlled in the attempt to achieve what is best for them.

The view that man is born good and is therefore perfectible through modern technology denies the biblical view that man is a sinner in history. It tends to make the divine secular, the eternal temporal, and the absolute relative. If the optimistic interpreter recognizes God at all, he emphasizes God's immanence in the historical process rather than His transcendence as Creator and immanence as Redeemer. Social action by autonomous man, including educational efforts and social legislation, will usher in a golden age in future history. The natural law of evolution (say the communists), unaided human effort, or the idea of an immanent God will guarantee progress to Utopia. Contemporary advocates of optimistic philosophies of history reflect the Renaissance and Enlightenment. They look upon the historical process as redemptive, culminating in a golden era secured through man's own activities.

Nontheistic Views

Karl Marx (1818–1883) has influenced modern society so much that one-third to one-half of the world's population is under the iron sway of rulers and parties that subscribe to his ideas. This son of a converted Jewish lawyer, while studying at the University of Berlin, joined the young Hegel-group there. But his alienation from Hegel's idea that reality is mental or spiritual is discernible in his Ph.D. dissertation on Democritus and Epicurus, Greek materialistic philosophers. He later embraced the materialism of Ludwig A. Feuerbach, who insisted that *"Der Mensch ist wass er isst"* (A man is what he eats). Marx thus inverted Hegel's insistence on the importance of the transmaterial reality by making matter in motion the ultimate.

Marx moved to Paris from Berlin in 1843 and began to read the works of such men as Adam Smith and David Ricardo, who made labor the main source of value. In 1844 Marx met Friedrich Engels, who gave Marx financial aid for the rest of his life. Marx borrowed from the utopian socialists the idea that the distribution of goods should be "from each according to his ability, to each according to his need." He was expelled from France in 1845 and went to Brussels, where in 1848 he wrote *The Communist Manifesto.* By 1849 he was in London, where he lived the rest of his life in relative poverty and did research in the British Museum.

Though Marx gave his interpretation of history the name "scientific socialism," it is, as later scholars have demonstrated, far from scientific in either data or presuppositions. Most of his ideas he borrowed from others. He borrowed Hegel's idea of development or philosophical evolution in history. He also took over Hegel's dialectic, the conception that progress comes through the development of contradictions, which through conflict resolve into a synthesis. This becomes the basis for another set of opposing forces to be resolved in a new synthesis. His idea that matter in motion is ultimate came mainly from Feuerbach. From the French physiocrats and Adam Smith he derived his concept that labor is the creator of value. His principle for the distribution of goods he took from French utopian socialists.

Thus Marx's main ideas in the philosophical realm were borrowed. He supported these ideas by a one-sided study of bad historical conditions in England during the industrial revolution. He had a keen sense of what was unjust. Despite his acerbic nature, he also had compassion for the poor, though he did little for them in his own day.

Marx believed that history, when scientifically studied, and philosophy provide the ideas that unify and explain history. Because matter in motion is the ultimate reality, economic forces determine the shape of social institutions, which always reflect the outlook of the ruling group. This was Marx's doctrine of historical materialism.

Because labor is the sole producer of value and because the capitalist gives the laborer only subsistence wages, there is a surplus value of profits that should go to labor but that goes instead to the capitalist, said Marx. Price should consist of wages alone. This surplus value enables the capitalist to become wealthy and to develop a monopolistic concentration of capital. The rich capitalist becomes richer and the poor worker poorer. A class struggle ensues in a dialectic that is the dynamic of social progress. The master-slave relationship in early society led to a conflict that resulted in the development of the feudal system. The lord-serf relationship in this system brought conflict that in turn precipitated the modern capitalistic system. In this system the capitalistic middle class clashes with the workers, the proletariat beloved of Marx.

The workers would be led by a professional revolutionary elite, who would sieze power in economic crisis or war and set up a temporary dictatorship of the proletariat. In time the state would inevitably wither away and a classless society would emerge in which each would produce what he could and receive what he needed. History is simply an economic process that will renovate the world through world revolution.

This sounds much like an inversion of Christian eschatology, according to which a kingdom of God will be established upon earth. This is why Toynbee labeled Marxism a Christian heresy. The kingdom of Marx is an earthly kingdom in time, and the chosen people in this kingdom are the proletariat. Marxism has no room for any motivation in history except the economic, and it lacks any ultimate except a temporal, earth-bound, historical process in motion. Man can live by bread alone, it contends, and religion is only an "opiate" that the ruling class uses to keep the proletariat content while exploiting them.

In many democratic, capitalistic countries production has been so great that the workers have a higher standard of living than Marx ever envisaged. He also had an unrealistic view of human nature: because man is born good, changing his environment will bring happiness. But this view ignores the universality of human sin and the sacredness of personality that is lost in the communist state. God is shut out from the historical process by atheism. Spiritual and ethical forces are neglected, while violence becomes a legitimate means to the ideal goal. Determinism gives Marx's view a grim inevitability, guaranteeing that the goal will be realized no matter how much slaughter and human suffering are necessary.

Idealistic and Theistic Views

Though Marx and other atheistic interpreters have no place for God in history, others view history as progressing from God as its source to God and an ideal order as its goal. **Giovanni Battista Vico** (1668–1744) offers an interesting combination of the view that history can be both scientifically studied and providentially guided.

Vico was the son of a bookstore owner in Naples. Young Vico was no stranger to poverty, being dogged by it all through life. At the age of seven he fell and crushed the right side of his skull, after which he was sick for three years. Tuberculosis more than once threatened his life and finally contributed to his death. He studied philosophy under the Jesuits, and after studying law he was admitted to the bar at age sixteen. He practiced law for a time until becoming a private tutor. Finally in 1699 he was named professor of rhetoric at the University of Naples and held that post until 1741, when his son succeeded him.

In 1725 he published the first edition of *New Science,* but it failed to bring him the fame he had hoped it would. This was the first major attempt to put the philosophy of history on a scientific basis. He drew on Francis Bacon and René Descartes for the scientific side of his work, but he opposed the general views of Descartes as inconsistent with Christian theology.

Because that which is true and that which is created are one, the creator can know that which he has made. Therefore God, the creator of nature and man, can know them. While man can never know nature as fully as God can, he can know history and find continuity in it. Man, after all, made history. For one who would know the human past, documents are most important, but history is also events ordered by Providence.

Vico held that history, which began when God created the world immediately rather than through an evolutionary process, is made up of a series of units or societies, each of which goes through a three-stage cycle. These three cycles, believed by Vico to have been "handed down to us" by the

Egyptians, are the age of the gods, the age of heroes, and the age of man. During the first age savage and cruel men live under divine command in a theocracy where knowledge comes by myth. During the second, courageous warrior aristocrats rule in pride and honor. And during the third, all men are equal and rational, governed by either popular commonwealths or able monarchs. The third age in the cycle will be followed by an age of barbarism, from which a new society will arise to go through the same, three-stage cycle and fall. These two latter he called *corsi* and *recorsi.* Every society is part of a spiral movement of ascent in which progress is possible and can be transmitted from one cycle to another.

Providence, although invisible, does "rule the affairs of men," but it does so with the gentilic nations in general and with the Jews in particular. Because the Jews had received special, divine revelation, Vico exempted them from his historic cycles. Only the gentilic nations go through these social cycles, which are under the control of general providence. This general providence does not seem to have been so much the work of a transcendent God as that of a being or reason in the process of history. Thus each cycle is not self-contained and relativistic as it is in Spengler's system. This invisible force or person, which is outside man but immanent in history, keeps sinful man from destroying himself.

Vico's method seems at home in the rationalistic eighteenth century, but he did not give up God as the philosophes did. Piety was a prerequisite to wisdom, and history, with its providentially guided cycles, had purpose for Vico. John W. Montgomery in *The Shape of the Past* helpfully developed the theistic aspect of Vico's work.[21] Vico thought he had built a Christian philosophy of history on a scientific foundation. He also believed he had created a scientific history through scientific methods, so that it was amenable to "laws." He wanted historians to avoid exaggerating the past, becoming nationalistic, or concluding that similarity in history always implies borrowing or diffusion.

The period from the French Revolution to the mid-nineteenth century has been called the Romantic Era because men subordinated reason to emotion, feeling, or sensibility as the guiding force in history. During this era idealistic thinkers such as Immanuel Kant, Johann Gottfried von Herder, and

21. Pp. 187–216.

Georg Hegel developed philosophies of history that see nature and nations as becoming or growing. One can best understand the present, they said, by studying its gradual growth and development as a genetic process rather than by studying it in the colder, analytical, scientific way so admired in the eighteenth century. Hegel is probably the best known of these idealistic philosophers of history, and he has greatly influenced both rightist and leftist twentieth-century totalitarianism.

Georg Hegel (1770–1831), building on the foundations laid by Kant and Herder, developed the most influential philosophy of history since the days of Augustine in *Lectures on the Philosophy of History* (1837), lectures delivered in 1831. Even as a boy Hegel did scholarly work, and in 1793 he graduated from Tübingen in philosophy and theory, although the examiners found him "weak in theology." After teaching at Jena and Heidelberg, he occupied the chair of philosophy at the University of Berlin from 1818 until his death.

Hegel spoke of history as original, reflective, and philosophical. Original history is contemporary, so one can have firsthand knowledge of most facts. Universal reflective history involves the study of the whole of history, tracing the history of a people or nation. It also involves the study of the past for didactic purposes (pragmatic history) and of the history of history (critical history). Hegel spoke of his work as the third kind, philosophical history, in which one works to interpret the whole rather than concentrates on details.

The idea, absolute, spirit, or mind seeks to develop itself in space and realizes this goal in nature. History is the development in time of the absolute in man towards freedom, as Hegel understood it.[22] The real is rational, and all that is rational is real. Hegel was "a kind of philosophic Augustine." His idea of history has also been described as "the autobiography of God."

History is as well a process of development[23] moving toward a complete consummation. Hegel thus advocated a kind of philosophic evolution in which the "cunning of Reason" guides historical progress through world heroes. The technique by which development takes place is the dia-

22. *Lectures on the Philosophy of World History,* trans. H. B. Nisbet (New York: Cambridge University, 1975), pp. 10, 13, 19–20, 26, 56, *476.*

23. Ibid., pp. 18, 24, 56, 57.

lectic. Something that exists in and of itself is the thesis, which is soon opposed by an antithesis or contradiction. The conflict is resolved in a higher synthesis of rational freedom. This process continues until the Idea becomes fully free, which is the goal of history. History is only the increasing consciousness of freedom as right and as the law in the state.[24] This is the end product, in which the world spirit is manifested or is the "divine Idea as it exists on earth." For Hegel all were free in the strong and just Prussian, Protestant, monarchical state.[25] In each case the absolute uses heroes, as Hegel called them, to realize a higher universal and to conform their times to the higher laws of the absolute.

The individual counted for little when Hegel applied the dialectic to history. In the first stage, the Orient, only the monarch was relatively free, ruling men despotically while himself sharing in the freedom of the absolute. In the antithesis, classical civilization, a few were free in an aristocratic society, but most were still in slavery. In the Germanic world, the synthesis, the Reformation had made men spiritually free in the state church, and the Enlightenment had freed their minds in the German state under law. This was the greatest realization of the Idea in history up to that time. It is little wonder that in this era of romanticism, men wrote national histories marked by deep feeling for their countries and spent much time and money filling national archives.

Hegel overgeneralized and oversimplified history, especially in his exaltation of the state. The state is not an organism but an aggregation of men coming together, with divine approval of the state, to avoid chaos. Hegel was also guilty, as historians often are, of chauvinism, putting Germany far above previous or contemporary states.

His glorification of the state was taken up by twentieth-century, right-wing totalitarians led by Benito Mussolini and Adolf Hitler, who thought of individuals as the means and the state as the end. Marx borrowed both Hegel's idea of philosophic development and his dialectic, but reversed Hegel's concept of mind as reality, making matter in motion the ultimate reality. Few men have had so great an impact on history as Hegel, with his secularized version of Christianity.

George Sherwood Eddy (1871–1963) in *God in History* (1947) reflected Heglian idealism and modern Darwinian evo-

24. Ibid., pp. 17, 24, 40–41, 43, 49, 52. 25. Ibid., pp. 19, 54.

lution. With the dialectic as his tool[26] and with education guaranteeing evolutionary progress, he felt that man can follow the example of Jesus. The emphasis of the United States on liberty and love and the emphasis of Russia on racial brotherhood and economic justice are the thesis and antithesis that will one day be synthesized in a worldwide "socialized planned economy" with "ideals of liberty and justice." These optimistic ideas grew out of Eddy's education, his experience as a Y.M.C.A. secretary, and his several visits to Russia. He is a clear example of the liberal, optimistic thinkers who see progress coming mainly through human effort, education, and legislation. He strangely ignored any role for the church in this process. Robert W. McLaughlin and Shailer Mathews also reflected liberal theology, critical biblical scholarship, evolution, and Hegelian thought in their books on the interpretation of history. Hegelian philosophy, Darwinian evolution, and biblical criticism seem to have been the stock in trade of these liberal historians before the hurricane of World War I destroyed their optimistic view of progress as the law of history.

Arthur W. Munk (1909–), influenced by personalists like Edgar S. Brightman, set forth in *History and God*[27] his view of a limited God. Presupposing both the animal origin of man by evolution and biblical criticism, Munk claimed that his rational and empirical study of history had revealed the following: (1) God, whose existence is the only explanation of time, natural law, and personality; (2) man's mind, his love and creation of beauty, and his moral and religious capacity; (3) the cruel, irrational, evil aspect of human nature; (4) evolutionary advances to unity and moral order in history; (5) apparent pattern; (6) the finitude of God, who is limited in power but is still the greatest force in the universe, and who is the "World Ground" that brings increasing order out of the chaos and evil in history; and (7) immortality, which is necessary to guarantee justice since goodness is often unrewarded in this world. Ecumenicity, a tenderer social conscience, and the United Nations are signs that God and man are together creating international unity and economic justice in the march toward the goal of history.

26. *God in History* (New York: Association, 1947), p. 13.

27. *History and God: Clues to His Purpose* (New York: Ronald, 1952).

Arnold J. Toynbee's (1889–1975) *Study of History*[28] is the most voluminous and influential of all attempts to write a philosophy of history. His *Civilization on Trial*[29] offers a briefer summary of his ideas. Most historians, however, do not accept Toynbee's scheme because they think his propositions are not supported by the empirical data.

Toynbee gained much of his love for history from his mother. He studied Greek and Latin classics at Winchester and at Balliol College. From November 1911 to August 1912 he hiked in Greece. Upon his return to England in 1912, he taught Byzantine and modern Greek history at King's College of the University of London. From 1925 on, he directed studies at the Royal Institute of International Affairs, but from 1939 to 1946 he devoted most of his time to directing the Research Department of the British Foreign Office. He wrote many books, lectured widely, and traveled all over the world.

In the first ten volumes of his twelve-volume work—which has fortunately been issued in an abridged, two-volume edition[30]—Toynbee claimed to have followed empirical, scientific techniques in studying history comparatively. He believed that his "laws" of history grew out of the data. When he studied any history, he found he could not stop with national or regional histories but had to return to civilizations as the basic unit in historical cycles.[31] This sounds like Spengler, but unlike him Toynbee was optimistic, believing that if man acts correctly, progress can be made in history.[32] Like Vico and unlike Spengler, Toynbee emphasized the role of religion in history. Man can have freedom in working out his destiny. Time is linear rather than cyclical.

In his earlier volumes Toynbee wrote of twenty-three civilizations that had come and gone. Five, like the Eskimo civilization, were abortive, and four were arrested civilizations. In a later volume he identified thirty-two civilizations, and in another instance he listed thirty-four.[33] These civilizations have originated in a successful response to the challenge of hard lands or outside foes. These challenges were not too

28. *A Study of History,* 12 vols. (London: Oxford University, 1934–1961).

29. *Civilization on Trial* (New York: Oxford University, 1948).

30. *A Study of History,* ed. D. C. Somervell, 2 vols. (New York: Oxford University, 1947–1957).

31. *Civilization on Trial,* p. 222.

32. *A Study of History,* 4:33–35; 6:324; 7:423.

33. Ibid., 12:558–61.

difficult but were near the golden mean of challenge.[34] Progress came in history as these civilizations moved to self-determination on ever higher levels of what Toynbee called etherialization. This is the process of moving from challenges that are material to those that are moral and spiritual.[35] This increasingly moves the earth and its people to a point where they become part of the kingdom of God. Civilization follows an upward line of growth.[36]

In successfully responding to challenge, people follow the lead of a creative minority through what Toynbee called mimesis or imitation. The leaders must periodically withdraw from their followers to renew the wellsprings of creativity. This seems to be in some respects an aristocratic approach to history.

The civilization begins to break down when the leadership loses its creativity. What was the creative minority becomes a dominant minority, maintaining its position by force in a universal state. The people separate from them in spirit and form an internal proletariat, finding solace in the development of a universal religion.[37] Meanwhile the civilization is threatened by the rise of an external, barbarian proletariat. The schism in society leads to internal weakness, making it an easy victim for the external proletariat. The universal religion then becomes the chrysalis[38] for a new civilization, which goes through the same process as its predecessor.[39] All civilizations are contemporaneous with each other in that they go through a similar cycle. They are destroyed from within by internal decay rather than from without by external forces. Toynbee stated that civilizations die by committing suicide. Theirs is a "self-inflicted destruction."[40]

Toynbee was not completely pessimistic about the future of contemporary Western civilization. He was hopeful that man would make the right choices to bring it through its time of troubles. Economic justice, an international state, and a universal religion must be established and developed. If they are, then man may not use atomic energy to destroy civiliza-

34. Ibid., 2:393.

35. Ibid., 3:128, 182ff.

36. *Civilization on Trial,* pp. 235–36, 244–45.

37. *A Study of History,* 1:99.

38. Ibid., 12:559.

39. *Civilization on Trial,* p. 13; *A Study of History,* 12:559.

40. *A Study of History,* 4:120; 8:527.

tion, and then civilization, which is now "a province of the Kingdom of God" in part, may become wholly that.[41]

The universal religion should be, according to Toynbee, a syncretism of Christianity and Mahayana Buddhism, each of which looks to an unselfish savior—Christ and Buddha, respectively—who voluntarily gave up immediate participation in the eternal to help their fellows. Toynbee insisted that no religion has a right to claim an exclusive written revelation of God's will.[42]

Toynbee was an agnostic concerning the existence of God. Having ceased to believe "in the doctrines of Christianity as an undergraduate,"[43] Toynbee said, "I don't know whether there is a God. . . ."[44] Thus his system is religious rather than Christian in its hope for a universal religion. He also followed modern biblical criticism in his conclusion that the Bible is myth and legend and that it is only one of several equally valid revelations of God's will. Archaeologists have shown that "it has to be taken with a grain of salt."[45] Toynbee's view of man led one historian to call his work "a Pelagian twentieth-century *City of God.*" Some feel that Toynbee ignored technological and economic forces in history, but he did acknowledge that Europe's superior technology was what had enabled it to bring under control the Western Hemisphere, Africa, and Asia.

Certain weaknesses are common to optimistic interpretations of history. These approaches to the human past stress inductive science or speculative reason, making them man-centered rather than God-centered. They generally fail to realize that progress so far has been mainly technological, intellectual, and organizational, and that man can pervert it to evil ends. Because of the inroads of biblical criticism, special revelation is so discounted that the Bible becomes only a historical book—fallible and subjective—to be studied like any other human book. Recognizing the universality of human sin but not its origin in original sin, these historians have a Pelagian concept of human nature. The glorious end of history in history will come by human educational and

41. *Civilization on Trial,* pp. 28, 39, 263; *A Study of History,* 7:558.

42. *A Study of History,* 7:428 (note 2).

43. G. R. Urban, ed., *Toynbee on Toynbee: A Conversation Between Arnold J. Toynbee and G. R. Urban* (New York: Oxford University, 1974), p. 38.

44. Ibid., p. 14.

45. Ibid., p. 8.

legislative effort. War and poverty will be eliminated, allowing all to live in prosperity and peace. This is the vision of the biblical prophets humanized and secularized. Christ is not the Lord of history who controls its course and destiny and who will finally resolve its problems when He comes the second time. But the humanistic tradition of the Renaissance and the naive belief that man is perfectible and can make indefinite progress through science dies hard.

Annotated Bibliography

Grace E. Cairns in *Philosophies of History* (1962) discussed in detail the use of cycles in philosophies of history through the ages. She tended too much to reduce all views of history to cyclic interpretations, however. Alan and Barbara Donagan in *Philosophy of History* (1965) summarized and offered well-chosen sources of the various philosophies of history. William H. Dray in *Philosophy of History* (1964) discussed in some depth the theories of Georg Hegel, Arnold J. Toynbee, and Reinhold Niebuhr. Karl Löwith thoughtfully discussed the main approaches of this chapter in *Meaning in History* (1949). By working back from Marx to Augustine and the Bible, Löwith showed how modern views of history are an inversion and secularization of the biblical conception. John W. Montgomery in chapter 4 of *The Shape of the Past* (1962) summarized and criticized modern and contemporary theories of history propounded by theistic, liberal, and neo-orthodox thinkers. Excellent introductions and relevant selections from the sources may be found in *Ideas of History* (1969) edited by Ronald H. Nash. *Theories of History* (1959) edited by Patrick Gardiner is a similar volume. Alban G. Widgery in *Interpretations of History* (1961) summarized very well these philosophies of history.

CHAPTER 7

Philosophies of History: Pessimistic-Optimistic

Both the pessimistic and optimistic interpreters of history have some helpful ideas. The pessimists rightly point to the recurrent parallels in successive historical eras and to the tragic element arising out of human frustration, failure, or old-fashioned sin. These parallels and failures in history are not, however, the result of determinism.

Optimistic interpreters correctly believe in human progress through technology and social institutions, but they forget that true progress includes moral and spiritual development that is impossible apart from common grace or the redemptive power of God. Because they insist that man is like Adam before the fall and is capable of becoming sinless, they develop "pitiful Pelagian programs" to help perfectible man create a final Utopia.

Pessimistic-optimistic interpreters, like the pessimists, accept the failure and frustration of sinful man in history, but they reject the determinism of the pessimists that leaves man without a ray of hope. They even admit a temporal cyclical tendency in history because sinful human nature is the same, no matter how different the time and space settings are. Because they believe man to be stained with sin from birth, they are not unduly optimistic concerning man in current history. Nor are they unduly pessimistic, due to their faith in God's grace in history. The idea of man transforming history by his own effort in history leaves them cold, but they do look for redemption by God in and at the end of history. They are confident that the purpose and grace of God guarantee an optimistic note in history, but they cannot accept the idea of indefinite human progress through education and legislation. Despair of history or undue hope of progress gives way to faith in God, which in turn results in the proclamation of salvation to society in the present and the practice of loving service. They do this with a hope for the future grounded in God, who transforms history through His Son, the Lord of history. At Christ's catastrophic coming the earth will become fully His kingdom. History is linear, and Jew, Muslim, and Christian view history as a straight line advancing to an eschatological objective, the kingdom of God.

Mediating Philosophies

Mediating interpreters in this category, like the neo-orthodox, reject both the authority of Scripture and its historicity. John Baillie wrote in *Invitation to Pilgrimage* of the "myth of the Garden of Eden."[1] These historians believe that universal sin is a historical fact, but that the story of Adam and Eve is only a tale describing this fact; there never was a historical Adam and Eve. They still believe, like the liberal, optimistic interpreter, in progress in history, but unlike the liberals they attribute this progress to man's being empowered by God.

Herbert Butterfield (1900–), who is almost as well-known an interpreter of history as Arnold J. Toynbee, best illustrates the approach to history taken by this group. Professor of modern history at Cambridge for most of his life, Butterfield, now retired, is a Methodist who seems to follow the liberal tradition.

His major work of historical interpretation is *Christianity and History.*[2] According to this volume, academic or tech-

1. *Invitation to Pilgrimage* (London: Oxford University, 1942), p. 53.

2. *Christianity and History* (New York: Scribner, 1950).

nical history, with its scientific methodology, is more valuable than a heroic type of contemporary history that sees everything in black and white terms. Technical history must, however, be supplemented by religious understanding to help explain the tragic in history.

Revelatory data must, wrote Butterfield, be considered by the historian in his final assessment. Sin is universal, and the human will is free to practice either evil or good.[3] Human personality exists for the glory of God and is important in history. Being spiritual in nature, it has spiritual autonomy as its end. For this reason man must be put above things.[4] Neither nations nor individuals should pass moral judgment upon each other; if they do, they will become self-righteous sinners who merit judgment.

The dynamic of history, Butterfield continued, is Christ's law of love rather than force or the state. This love is seen in the "suffering Servant" of the Old Testament. Suffering perfects love.[5] (While Butterfield said much about love and about Christ's example of that love, he is strangely silent concerning Christ's substitutionary work on the cross.) Because of sin men face interim judgment within history as well as final judgment at the end of history.[6] Germany's sufferings after World War II, for example, were judgment for her pride and presumption under Adolf Hitler.

Butterfield concluded that the real purpose of history is to make and educate human souls.[7] Nations can best serve one another by maintaining a balance of power and, if war becomes necessary, by limiting its scope instead of engaging in a total war. In spite of evil, man can do much to improve his external situation.[8]

Butterfield's insight into the value of human personality, which is developed in history in the education of souls for eternity, is valid. So too is his belief that scientific study of the past on the horizontal level needs to be supplemented by a verbal revelatory element for history to be understandable. His final word is commendable: "Hold to Christ, and for the rest be totally uncommitted."[9] But the role in history that he assigns to Scripture and Christ is too weak.

3. Ibid., pp. 29, 34, 35, 38, 39, 41, *42, 45,* 63, 106.
4. Ibid., pp. 29, 67, 112.
5. Ibid., p. 86.
6. Ibid., pp. 48–67, esp. 50, 52, 60, 66.
7. Ibid., pp. 76, 112.
8. Ibid., pp. 63, 96–97, 112.
9. Ibid., p. 146.

John Baillie (1886–1960) in *The Belief in Progress*[10] placed progress in a providential framework. After critically depicting the idea of progress at length,[11] he advanced the view that man can make moral and spiritual progress in history in the interim between Christ's two comings to earth.[12] This comes about as technology gives him control of nature and as institutions relate him peacefully to his fellows in society.[13] Because men are sinful and because technology and institutions can be used for evil as well as good, God must be the ground for progress. Though the end of history is beyond history,[14] God will aid men by linking their wills with His, meaning that His Spirit will be progressively embodied in man and society.[15] Personal salvation, renewal of social life, and final salvation at the end of history come through Christianity. Thus progress is possible through the power of God in man, but it is not inevitable because men are sinful and free to choose evil as well as good. Baillie retained a degree of pessimism due to sin, but he believed that man can triumph in history through Christ.

Kenneth Scott Latourette (1884–1968), a specialist in Far Eastern history and missions, was even more specific about the possibility of progress—mainly spiritual progress—between the two advents of Christ. In *The Unquenchable Light*[16] Latourette visualized progress in history as alternate advances and recessions. Each advance reaches a higher point than the preceding one, and each recession is less pronounced than the previous one. There have been four recessions, the last beginning in 1914, and four eras of advance, the greatest lasting from 1815 to 1914. Latourette called the latter era the "great century" of missions and devoted three volumes of his history of missions to it. Increases in geographical spread, in number of adherents, in power of Christian movements, and in the impact of Christianity on civilizations are the yardsticks Latourette used to assess the advance of Christianity.

Latourette set forth these ideas in 1948 in his presidential address to the American Historical Association. In this

10. *The Belief in Progress* (London: Oxford University, 1951).

11. Ibid., pp. 1–154.

12. Ibid., pp. 190, 214.

13. Ibid., pp. 176–77.

14. Ibid., p. 183.

15. Ibid., pp. 189–90, 210, 220.

16. *The Unquenchable Light* (New York: Harper, 1941).

paper, titled "The Christian Understanding of History,"[17] he substituted the sovereignty of God and man's value to God for deterministic cyclical views and linear conceptions of inevitable progress.[18] Christianity reveals its power in the geographical, moral, and social influence it wields, as for example in helping to end slavery. This process will continue to the end of history, in which there is a "strong probability" that God will fully triumph over sin. Of the mediating views under discussion in this section, Latourette's comes closest to that of a biblical theist. But one senses in him much of the liberal optimism that confidently predicted Christianity's triumph in history through man.

These moderate interpreters of history all depict spiritual progress in time as the result of the church being present in society and empowered by Christ. They renounce limitless progress in history, but with the exception of Latourette they fail to make clear the role of Christ in history. While they are conscious of sin's power, they remain optimistic that with divine aid man can overcome it in history.

Neo-orthodox Philosophies

Neo-orthodox interpreters owe much to Karl Barth, who in turn was influenced by Sören Kierkegaard and the earlier German idealistic philosophers. Impressed with the diabolic and intractable nature of events surrounding World War I, Barth turned to Calvinism and Paul's Epistle to the Romans. There he found an answer that was far less shallow than the naive evolutionary optimism of Liberalism, which elevated reason, advocated human perfectiblity, and guaranteed progress. Thus Barth's was an intellectual and spiritual revolt against the cult of reason and progress, according to which God is immanent in each man. Neo-orthodoxy has been influential in the United States through the writings of such men as Reinhold Niebuhr, Otto Piper, and Paul Tillich, but it is now losing its grip.

When these men applied their theology to a philosophy of history, they found a discontinuity in history, a dualism of salvation history on the divine level and scientific history on the human level. Faith and history are thus separated. The

17. "The Christian Understanding of History," *The American Historical Review* 54 (1949): 259–76.

18. Ibid., p. 266.

neo-orthodox are looked on for this reason as somewhat anti-historical. Revelation for them is not in the propositions or words of the Bible, but in the instances recorded there of God's intervention in history—events such as the exodus, the incarnation, and the death and resurrection of Christ. The Bible is not the objective, inspired, historical Word of God but only a witness to the acts of God. It is subject to error, containing "myths" to enshrine historical facts. In the human crisis in which God confronts the human soul, the Bible can become the Word of God to the individual by the activity of the Holy Spirit. Except for Niebuhr these man had little interest in social action and rejected the liberal idea of progress on earth. Barth told the founding assembly of the World Council of Churches, meeting in Amsterdam during 1948, that the "care of the world is not the care of the church." They also disavow apologetics and depreciate reason, believing that God is transcendent above history and not immanent in it.

All of these ideas represent a reaction against Liberalism and an attempt to put history on a more solid basis. The neo-orthodox historians did, however, accept the ideas of biblical criticism. The Bible, which becomes the Word of God, contains error and myth. Too often biblical truth dissolves into symbols. Neo-orthodox men also held in most cases to biological and social evolution. Christ's incarnation, death, and resurrection lose historical meaning in the neo-orthodox frame of reference.

Reinhold Niebuhr (1892–1971) has been one of the most influential neo-orthodox thinkers in the United States. A pastorate of thirteen years among assembly-line workers in a Detroit suburb and the study of Marxism made him much more interested in social action than were others who were neo-orthodox. Teaching at Union Seminary in New York, beginning in 1928, helped to mature his ideas. He set forth his view of history in *Faith and History*.[19] Man is both a "creature and creator of history," knowing both necessity and freedom. Because he is finite and fallen and because sin is universal, man can accomplish no good apart from God. But history can be a redemptive process.[20] Due to the universality of sin, history would be meaningless without Christ's life,

19. *Faith and History: A Comparison of Christian and Modern Views of History* (New York: Scribner, 1949).

20. Ibid., p. 2.

death, and resurrection, in which God took man's sin upon Himself. Man becomes related to God when in crisis he is confronted with God's claims upon him and takes the leap of faith. This act of faith gives unity to history, although man can neither claim moral perfection nor solve the problems of history by progress and human effort. Man's capacity and his "cultural achievements and social institutions" are capable of continued though finite development because man is creative and in some sense a creator of history.[21] Through love made actual in deeds, the Christian can bring about in time, in a limited way, a Christian social order, but he cannot create in history a perfect order. Final judgment at the end of history comes from outside history. It is the act of God by which time ends in eternity.[22] Apart from Niebuhr's concept of limited social progress in time, his ideas are quite typical of neo-orthodox philosophies of history. Historical truth discovered by scientific methods must be supplemented by final truth and meaning that come by faith.

Nikolai Berdyaev (1874–1948) was in the same tradition. In *The Meaning of History*[23] he too separated world history from sacred history. He pictured the West in the last stage of an era that started with the Renaissance. During this period nature and redemption had been unwisely separated, and man, having been identified with nature, had become a means. The theory of the natural rights of man had ended the unity of his spiritual life and left him open to a history of tragedy and conflict. God, who has a primal dark abyss in His nature, did create the world. The dark abyss in His nature is shared with man, who is His creation. History is thus both terrestrial and celestial. Although free to create and to put spiritual before material ends, man lost his higher nature by immersing himself in physical nature. The incarnation and the cross show that there is tragedy and suffering in the nature of God, and God shares with man the tragedy of free yet fallen life. Celestial history pierces terrestrial history through Christ, and man and God can move in spiritual fellowship to an eternal, eschatological end outside human history. Eternity will bring about the resolution of tragedy in man and God. Berdyaev thought his view to be better than the West's selfish individualism or Russia's impersonal state

21. Ibid., pp. 70–74.

22. Ibid., pp. 232, 235.

23. *The Meaning of History* (London: Bles, 1936).

collectivism. It is, however, a manifestation of the Russian mystic's brooding approach.

In *Christ and Time*[24] **Oscar Cullman** (1902–) pictured Christ as the midpoint or center of history and described eternity as a continuous time process in which salvation takes place. His high view of Christ and His work, however, fails to free him from such neo-orthodox ideas as subjectivism, the distinction between the Word of God and the Bible, and the reduction of eternity to unending time.

George A. Buttrick (1892–) offered a more popular interpretation of history in *Christ and History.*[25] He called Oswald Spengler's pessimistic view of history a "circular prison" or treadmill, and he opposed the earlier liberals' optimistic view that history is an escalator. History is for Buttrick a dialogue instituted by God between Himself and man-in-pilgrimage, using the medium of events or divine acts. God had to initiate the dialogue because of man's brokenness and failure. God reveals Himself in actions or events rather than in words or propositions. History is repetitive but unique, as with the incarnation; purposeful but irrational, as with natural disasters; progressive but retrogressive, as with nuclear bombs. History becomes meaningful only in an act of faith by the individual. Its end is beyond itself through the activity of the divine Christ, who comes into history from above history. Scientific history cannot account for salvation history.

Many other neo-orthodox thinkers might be considered, but these four are typical. Their stress on the universality of sin, on God's transcendence and holiness, and on the weakness of reason, and their denial of the modern cult of progress make them more realistic and less naive than the previous liberal movement.

They are deficient, however, in their intrusion of a dualism in history that denies the unity and continuity of history under Christ's Lordship. God may be transcendent over His creation, but He is certainly immanent in it, creatively and redemptively active. Ambiguous, often symbolic views of Christ's cross and resurrection weaken Neo-orthodoxy and lead to a denial of His historical reality and work. Apolo-

24. *Christ and Time: The Primitive Christian Conception of Time and History,* trans. Floyd V. Filson (Philadelphia: Westminster, 1950).

25. *Christ and History* (New York: Abingdon, 1963).

getics is impossible with the neo-orthodox denial of reason and in some cases its mystical, subjective outlook. Except for Niebuhr, the neo-orthodox had little sense of man's social responsibility to his fellows. The destructive biblical criticism that they accepted left them with a Bible that can only become the Word of God in crisis, rather than a Bible that is an objective, historical word from God. Belief in universal election seems to have led some to a belief in universal salvation. Though their philosophies of history are more realistic than those of the optimists, they fail to do justice to either the biblical or the historical data. Man is left helpless in secular history unless God pierces history through an event or divine act.

Historic Evangelical Philosophies

Though the Bible points out instances of cyclical recurrence (Eccles. 1:4–11), evangelical interpreters of history have seen this as referring to the regularity of nature guaranteed by Providence, rather than to recurrence in history as the Greeks conceived it. Although holding to a linear view of history, evangelical interpreters have not viewed progress as the fruit of human labor alone, but as the result of God guiding history to a cataclysmic end. Divine intervention is what guarantees hope for man at the end of history. Neither pessimism nor progress by human effort can adequately explain historical phenomena or relate them to ultimate meaning. Eighteenth-century liberals and the communists have inverted the Christian view when they have sought the solution to history inside the process instead of in God outside the process. They have found the end of history in a relative, temporal, human millennium upon earth, ushered in by human effort. History for them is an "ascending road of human progress."

Evangelical interpreters have insisted that history is teleological, replete with meaning, purpose, and goal. Each event of scientific history is in some way related to the whole in a linear progression. Scientific methodology supplies the data of knowledge and even some valid inductions, but it cannot relate the part to the whole. Only if the Christ of the Scriptures becomes the Lord of history does historical data make sense. Men such as Augustine, Otto of Freising, Jacques B. Bossuet, and, in America, Jonathan Edwards have insisted that revealed data must be considered along with scientifically acquired historical data. Justin Martyr in his *Dialogue with Trypho,* Origen in his *Against Celsus,* and Augustine in *The City of God* all repudiated cyclical conceptions of history.[26] They, like the Jewish writers, insisted that history is fraught with religious significance and that historic progression reveals something of the design and direction of God's will, which is revealed more specifically in the Bible. To them all history is one.

The classic postbiblical expression of this approach to history, the one that has influenced all pessimistic-optimistic interpreters, is found in *The City of God.* **Augustine** (354–430) wrote this book at the request of Marcellinus after the Visigoths, led by Alaric, sacked the city of Rome in 410. This event seemed cataclysmic to the Romans, who had controlled the city for nearly 1,500 years. Augustine's task was to show that this catastrophe had not happened because the Romans had forsaken their gods for the God of Christianity. Augustine got his student and friend Orosius to write *Seven Books of Histories Against the Pagans* to show that Rome's troubles were the result instead of their sins; indeed Rome's past history had more of blood, gloom, and doom before the Romans professed Christianity than after. Freed from this historical task, Augustine began work on a theological-philosophical treatment of universal history. Fourteen years later, in 426, he completed the manuscript. History is neither deterministic nor a meaningless cycle; it is under the divine sovereignty.

The first ten books of *The City of God* deal with the problem of whether or not one should serve the Roman gods. Augustine developed in books 1–5 the biblical and philosophical arguments against the view that temporal prosperity depends on worshiping pagan deities. In books 6–10 he argued that one does not have to give allegiance to pagan deities to enjoy spiritual benefits now and in the future. The final twelve books he devoted to the development of his philosophy of history.

The *creation* of the historical process is willed by a sovereign, self-sufficient God.[27] The universe and man are the result of God's special creative acts in time instead of the

26. *Dialogue with Trypho,* chap. 5; *Contra Celsum,* 4:67–68; 5:20–21; *The City of God,* 12:11, 14, 17.

27. *The City of God,* 5:1, 8–11; 12:14.

culmination of a long, evolutionary process. Because of special creation, man is a spiritual as well as material being, capable of communion with God.

The *compass* or scope of history was for Karl Marx the proletariat and for Georg Hegel the absolute state as an earthly manifestation of the absolute. Augustine's outlook was much broader. The scope of history is a unitary race made one by divine creation. It is broader than any city, nation, class, or culture.[28] This unity gave way to a temporal dualism in history when Adam and Even fell and sin entered the world. Since then the human race has been divided into the City of Earth and the City of God. In book 14, chapter 28, which seems to be the key to Augustine's work, he asserted that those in the former city love self, those in the latter love God first and above all else. These two cities are not church and state, as many medieval thinkers seemed to believe. In spite of Augustine's emphasis on the unity of the race, he acknowledged the importance to God of each individual.

Discussion of the origin and scope of history in books 11–14 is followed by a description of the *course* of history in books 15–18. Although Augustine confessed he did not know how to define time,[29] he vigorously opposed the classical idea of time as circular or cyclical.[30] He argued instead for a linear view that allows for God's redemptive activity on man's behalf. Christ was no disembodied, impersonal logos but a living person who was manifested in history. Augustine accepted cultural and technological progress,[31] but he had no patience with a spiral concept of progress, in which the church works for human betterment. Augustine divided into seven ages[32] the entire span of history, from the beginning of time to the end. This age is the sixth, and it is the millennium;[33] during this era the church actively engages in the personal, social, and cosmic struggle against evil. Although Augustine had a linear view of time with Christ at the center, he believed that there are periods of special divine activity in human history.

The temporal dualism of history, represented by the two cities, will give way to the cataclysmic *consummation* of his-

28. Ibid., 12:21, 27.

29. *Confessions,* 11:14.

30. *The City of God,* 12:11–14, 17.

31. Ibid., 22:24.

32. Ibid., 22:30.

33. Ibid., 20:7, 9.

tory, when Christ comes again, the dead are resurrected, and all men are judged. Then will begin the final period, the eternal age of divine rule. The saints will participate in this rule.

Augustine's view influenced later medieval and even modern thinkers, and few have developed an approach to human history as majestic as his. One who admitted his dependence on Augustine's general system was Otto of Freising.

Otto (1113?–1158), bishop of Freising, published the *Chronicle of the Two Cities* between 1143 and 1147. He was the nephew of Frederick II and grandson of Henry II, great German emperors, but chose a career in the church. He later became head of an abbey and was finally consecrated as a bishop.

Otto covered universal history from Adam to 1146 in eight books, the last of which is distinctly eschatological. He stated that he had followed "most of all those illustrious lights of the church, Augustine and Orosius," taking from them what was useful for his theme and purpose.[34] He wrote that the historian must avoid "certain things" and "select and arrange properly" the rest, for history "avoids lies and selects the truth." He added that he had recorded only what he had found "in the writings of trustworthy men," had heard from "credible men," or had "seen and heard" himself.[35]

In his first book Otto traced history down to the days of Romulus in Rome; in the next six, down to 1146. In the final book he described eschatological events linked with the coming of Christ.[36] Unlike Augustine at this point, Otto gave much detail from Scripture, and he interpreted it in a somewhat amillennial fashion. He built his scheme of history on the five-kingdom concept of Daniel,[37] using it to describe the course of the two cities. He wrote about the Babylonian, Persian, Greek, and Roman kingdoms and pictured the Holy Roman Empire of his day as a continuation of the Roman Empire, which had Latin, Frankish, and German phases. History moves westward and ends with the stone-cut-without-hands phase, which Otto thought is the final kingdom of

34. *Chronicle of the History of Two Cities,* prologue.

35. Ibid., 7:11.

36. Ibid., 8:7, 9, *13.*

37. Ibid., dedication; 2:13.

Christ upon earth. Until that event history is a tale of misery in war and of instability.

Otto believed that Christ's coming was near in his time[38] and that this event would end history, "the tale of human miseries." He thought the study of history would "make men live better in the fear of God." He confessed that he wrote the book in "bitterness of spirit." Human history, which had begun in the East, was coming to an end in the West. But the "city of Christ" was "not shaken" by the "misfortunes and tempests of the world." He had high praise for the Roman Empire, which had provided universal peace under Augustus, in whose reign Christ was born.

Otto's eschatology is much more detailed than Augustine's. Otto described a falling away and the revelation of Satan and Antichrist, who will persecute the church for three and a half years. Then the Jews will be converted and the evil city destroyed. Heaven and earth will pass away, and the dead will be raised at Christ's coming. After the final judgment the good will enjoy eternal bliss and the wicked will endure eternal punishment, which Otto described in lurid detail.

Jacques B. Bossuet (1627–1704), bishop of Meaux, also followed the Augustinian tradition in his *Discourse on Universal History* (1681). He tutored the son of Louis XIV and wrote this volume to instruct his royal pupil. His chosen people seems to be those in the Roman Catholic church. He covered history chronologically from creation to the reign of Charlemagne, giving special attention to the true religion. His work is centered on Christ's second advent rather than His incarnation. Empires fall in succession, but religion carries on through all changes by inherent power.

After giving a chronological epitome of events, dividing history into twelve epochs, Bossuet took up in the second part the history of religion in the Bible until the union of Jew and the church in Christ. The last part relates the succession of empires to the church. Although he thought primarily from a supernatural viewpoint, he did admit the presence of secondary factors in human affairs. He is in the tradition of Eusebius of Caesarea with his view of the triumphant church in time. God is in control of history for His glory and for the good of the church.

38. Ibid., 2:13; 6:36; 7:9, 34.

Not many are aware that **Jonathan Edwards** (1703-1758) planned to write a Christian philosophy of history. His life was cut short by a smallpox vaccination one month after he became president of Princeton. Such a work might well have ranked with that of Augustine because Edwards is considered one of America's greatest thinkers.

Edwards's *History of the Work of Redemption,* which was published posthumously, grew out of a series of sermons on the design of history and God's role in it. His central theme was the work of God in redeeming the elect, which Edwards thought is "the greatest of all God's works" and to which all else in history is related. The Jews were dispersed to make the facts about the Messiah more widely known. The Bible is the main historical source book. The period from man's fall into sin, which left him a sinner by both heredity and choice, to the incarnation was preparatory to the story of the redemption of the elect. During the era from the incarnation to the resurrection of Christ, the salvation of the elect was procured. The era from the resurrection to the consummation is marked by the success of God's plan for the elect.

"The work of redemption is the greatest of all God's works . . . , and it is the end of all His other works. . . ."[39] Creation and Providence show Christ's love for the elect. God, not "blind chance," governs the world. Because Christ's life and work are the center of history, all that preceded Christ was preparatory and all that has followed Him looks back to Him. Christ will finally come to take the elect He has redeemed and to judge the others. Then the church will be with Him forever.

Augustine, Otto, Bossuet, and Edwards all had a deep sense of man's failure in the Garden of Eden and since that time. They also rejected cyclical, pessimistic determinism and optimistic, linear views according to which unaided man can mold his own future and work out his salvation in the historical process. They were optimistic about the outcome of history because it is controlled by Christ the Redeemer, who will judge men at the end of history. They took into account both the data produced by scientific study and the revelatory data derived from Scripture.

39. *A History of the Work of Redemption,* period 3, section 4, part 10, 3.

Annotated Bibliography

C. A. Patrides traced the Christian philosophy of history from the Bible to the present, employing a wealth of scholarly data, in *The Grand Design of God* (1972).

CHAPTER 8

A Philosophy of History: Contemporary and Christian

Any honest historian will concede that there are two levels of history. There is the academic, technical, or scientific level, which is the result of carefully studying documents related to past events in order to make inductions. When they work on this horizontal, human level of historical study, both secular and Christian historians obtain similar results.

The second is the ultimate, divine, revelatory level. Secular historians root their ultimate in an absolute nature or in man. The Christian historian, however, realizes that a revelatory element must be taken into account; absolute truth exists, and is guaranteed by the existence of a personal, self-sufficient, sovereign God. The Christian historian neither rejects nor tries to explain away these facts because history makes no sense without them. How else can one explain Christ Himself, or the apparent indestructibility of the Jew in history, or the presence of evil in history, or the transformed persons in the church who live so differently from those around them? Thus any adequate interpretation of history must face the implications of the divine as well as the scientific element in history. The former, which comes from divine revelation in the Bible, cannot be absolutely proved by scientific methods, but it does provide a general principle of interpretation.

Archaeology has demonstrated that the Bible is an accurate historical record. Much of the Bible was written not as a historical record but as something with contemporary functional value. As an unconscious record, however, its value to the historian is even greater, and archaeological findings have uniformly upheld the veracity of its historical details.

Any historian who tries to find any meaning at all in his data accepts at least implicitly the idea of some final factor in history, whether economics, geography, great men, the proletariat, the absolute, or God. The historian must also explain recurrence (continuity) and change (the unique), both of which are present in historical data. Commitment to God frees him from nationalism, liberalism, and determinism in his work. Ultimate meaning is before, in, and beyond history.

The Creation or Source of History

A Christian historian can never be as pessimistic as some are about the presence of evil, the frustration of man, or the absence of final progress in history. Neither can he be as optimistic as are those who see man as autonomous and perfectible. The Christian will have a degree of pessimism about history in the short run because he sees evil as something rooted in the nature of man, not as a corrupting influence in the environment that can be eliminated by education or legislation. He will, however, counterbalance this short-run pessimism with a long-run optimism, basing it on the belief that God intrudes into history for the good of man. He follows in the tradition of Paul, Augustine, Otto of Freising, and Jonathan Edwards, who took the Bible as seriously as the data they derived from the careful study of documents. They realized that, as suggested in Deuteronomy 29:29, Psalm 115:16, and Amos 3:7, some things man can learn only from God's revelation in the Bible, while others, such as science and history, can be learned through a simple, scientific methodology. Both are necessary for a full-orbed interpretation of history.

Because any view of the creation is ultimately an act of faith that goes beyond the data, the Christian historian thinks of creation as an act in time of a transcendent, self-existent, and self-sufficient Person who wills to display His power (Rom. 1:20). He must be transcendent or, as a part of His creation, He shares in its limitations. On the other hand, He must be immanent in Providence and redemption, the eighteenth-century Deists notwithstanding. God is the source of all created things (Rom. 11:36; I Cor. 8:6; Eph. 4:6).

Applied science in technology has given man a large measure of control over nature, but too often he has used this technology and institutions to control his fellows, developing a culture that ignores God. Creation is not a continuing, cyclical process, nor is it one in which God is evolving with and in His creation to a higher form of reality. Scientific postulates of uniformity and design in nature offer empirical evidence that creation is the act of a supreme intelligence. God is the source and ground of reality.

The Bible insists on this point in passage after passage. Nature is the product of divine action (Gen. 1:1, 28; Pss. 8:3, 6; 19:1; 24:1–2; Isa. 40:26, 28; 42:5; 45:12; Jer. 27:5; Acts 14:15; 17:24; Rom. 1:20; I Cor. 8:6; Heb. 1:1–2; 11:3; Rev. 4:11), and Christ is the causative agent in this creation (John 1:1–3; Col. 1:16–17; Heb. 1:1–3).

Man, the chief actor on the stage of world history, is also the result of an act of divine creativity rather than of chance or a long process of evolution from lower forms of life. Moses (Gen. 1:26–2:25), Job (Job 33:4), the psalmist (Pss. 8:4–6; 90; 139:14–16), Isaiah (Isa. 42:5; 43:7; 45:12), Jeremiah (Jer. 27:5), and Paul (Acts 17:25–26) all categorically asserted that man came into being by a creative act of God in historic time.

After creating man, God gave him the task of mastering nature (Gen. 1:28; Ps. 8:6–8), for man's good and God's glory. This divine commission, often referred to as the cultural mandate, is the ground for man's scientific study of nature. Francis Bacon saw this clearly, writing in *Novum Organum* (1620) that the scientific method which he was describing is the tool man can use to carry out this mandate. History thus becomes a linear, divinely guided process with a meaningful end, instead of a meaningless, deterministic series of identical cycles or an evolutionary escalator carrying man and his world to perfection through applied science.

This is not to say that biblical writers of history did, or that modern Christian historians should, ignore the place of secondary, contingent, or conditional causes like economics, geography, or great men. Moses, Christ, and Paul, for example, gave place to the economic factor in history (Deut. 8:3; Matt. 4:4; I Thess. 4:11–12).

The Compass or Scope of History

Most historical interpreters have had a very provincial outlook. Karl Marx idealized his beloved proletariat as the ones who would achieve a classless, perfect society; Georg Hegel did something similar with the Prussian, Protestant, monarchical state. Biblical writers, and with them the Christian historian, consider history a universal and unitary process that involves the whole human race. All men are linked with Adam, who is the head of the race in its present state (Acts 17:26; Rom. 5:12–19). Fallen man has tried often to regain this unity in his own way. Alexander the Great, Julius Caesar, Charlemagne, Napoleon Bonaparte, Adolf Hitler, and the Communists under Joseph Stalin have all tried to establish a worldwide empire.

Temporal dualism in history, caused by human sin, is an empirical factor that the historian must take into account. Sin entered the human race when Adam and Eve failed to obey God's command in the garden. Instead they listened to the blandishment of Satan, who had earlier sinned by choosing to exalt his will above God's (Isa. 14:12–14; Ezek. 28:11–19). This fall brought the dualism into history of good and bad persons and left man with a corrupted nature that seems to blast all his efforts and corrupt what he touches (Gen. 3; Ps. 51:5; Jer. 9:17; 13:23; 17:9; Rom. 3:10, 23; 5:12–19; I Cor. 15:22; Eph. 2:2–3; I John 2:15–16). Even nature was affected by man's fall and longs for freedom from limitation and frustration (Gen. 3:17; Rom. 8:22–23). Because of the fall, the flesh, the call of the world, and the incitement of Satan, all men, who are sinful by nature, become guilty of actual sin as well.

In addition to his *fallenness,* which severely limits man's best instincts for good, man possesses *freedom* either to serve God or to serve evil and satisfy his selfish interests. Augustine wrote in *The City of God* that man's misuse of his will, serving self rather than God or others, is the very essence of sin and leads to frustration in history.[1] Sin is self-assertion in opposition to the will of God and the best interests of others.

Man is also characterized by *finitude,* although sometimes in his pride he claims to have ultimate knowledge. Paul was acutely conscious of how little man really knows and how clouded his view of reality in this life really is (I Cor. 13:12–14). Man is subject to physical, intellectual, and spiritual limitations that prevent him, apart from the grace of God, from ever achieving his goals.

Man experiences not only finitude but also *fallibility* in any kind of work or moral endeavor. No one is more conscious of how easy it is to err than is the truly educated man. If it were not for this fallibility, history would not need to be rewritten nor would the "sure results" of one generation of scientists have to be given up by a later generation. This is why personal and societal utopian schemes, when divorced from God, seem uniformly to end in failure.

This dualism in history surfaces in the clash between the Hellenic tradition of reason and the Hebraic tradition of faith. Men have tried to overcome this dualism by developing political or economic "new orders." Only Islam, Zoroastrianism, and Judaism have held that this dualism is temporal and will be resolved when a divine being comes in a cataclysmic manner and restores earth and redeemed man to their pristine state. This view does not exclude progress through technology, which gives man control over the environment, nor even a limited amount of cultural and moral progress. When men remember this, they do not idolize one of their fellows, their institutions, or even nature. Christianity alone offers the historian an explanation of the problem of evil in history.

The Course or Scheme of History

Paul believed the pattern of history to be under the control of God (Rom. 11:36; Eph. 4:6). Nothing could happen in nature or history without God's being aware of it. Why then does God not intervene in history to end war, racial injustice, economic injustice, and inequality in general? The reason is that God has granted man a will that is free, within divine limitations, to act in history. Eventually in His time and plan

1. 14:28.

God will again sovereignly intervene in history through His Son, as He did when Christ came the first time.

Divine Intervention in Nature

The creation of nature and its uniformity, without which science would be impossible, is the work of Christ (John 1:1–3; Col. 1:17; Heb. 1:3). The universe is made to cohere or is sustained by Providence in the form of natural law. What about natural calamities, which apparently contradict this idea? Historian Herbert Butterfield, like the biblical writers, considers them evidences of God's interim judgment in history, intended to bring men to repentance (Joel 1:4; 2:23–26). Other calamities may well result from man's violating order in nature. The barren wastelands of modern North Africa are the fruit of man's ravishing the soil in what was once the bread-basket of the Roman world. Many floods are caused by his denuding the hills of their forest cover.

God does, as Paul insisted, make known His power and deity through His creation (Rom. 1:19–20), but especially through His providence in the form of natural law, and even through His occasional miraculous interventions on man's behalf. God may thus be thought of as intervening in nature by law and even by special action, as when Christ performed miracles.

Divine Intervention in Other Ways

God also intervenes in history in other ways, which can often be seen empirically by the historian.

1. Human institutions are, according to biblical writers, products of the will or acts of God. The family, the basic unit of society, resulted from God's creative activity (Gen. 1:28; 2:20; Deut. 4:7–10; Matt. 19:4–6; Eph. 6:4). Societies that have allowed the family to decay or to depart from its original purpose have soon been relegated to the scrap heap of history.

God instituted government to promote order among men and to avoid anarchy and chaos (Gen. 9:5–6; Rom. 13:1–7; I Peter 2:13–17). The Bible endorses no particular form of government, but it does insist that society be organized so that law and order might prevail among sinful men. It provides for human cooperation for the enhancement of personality.

2. Human conscience, which presupposes a lawgiver, furnishes more evidence of divine activity in time (John 8:9; Rom. 2:15). People everywhere, as C. S. Lewis so ably pointed out, have some concept of a conscience that is triggered by an ethical code. This code originates not with custom but in an area beyond man's understanding of morality.

3. Moral values as well as conscience derive from God. The Ten Commandments, given to Moses on Mt. Sinai, speak of moral law as absolute, rooted in the moral nature of God rather than in the relativistic, changing customs of society. It is something that makes man conscious of what sin really is (Gal. 3:23–25). This moral law becomes the basis for interim judgment upon individuals and nations that transgress the rights of others. Butterfield views the catastrophe in Germany at the end of World War II as an example of interim judgment. No nation should rejoice when another nation falls because all are equally under moral law, as well as under the law of nations, which is rooted in morality. Perhaps this is why evil conduct is in the long run self-destructive. History provides examples of nations that have trampled upon the rights of other nations, only to fall themselves eventually.

4. Biblical prophecies that have been fulfilled also reveal divine action in history. Old Testament writers many times made prophecies that only came to fruition in Christ's life and work, such as Micah's prediction of where the Messiah would be born (5:2). In fact Isaiah challenged pagan gods to tell the future as his God did (Isa. 41:21–23; 42:9; 46:10; 48:3). Even when these biblical prophecies have been pared down to a minimum, there are still several whose integrity and authorship are not doubted even by liberal scholars. Otto of Freising was attracted to Daniel's graphic prophetic account of the course of Gentile history (Dan. 2). These prophecies offer data with which any honest historian must come to grips unless he takes the easy way out by denying prophecy.

5. God also sovereignly controls the events of history, particularly those relating to Gentile nations, Jews, and the Christian church (I Cor. 10:32). Daniel even linked supernatural beings such as angels with the course of human history (Dan. 10:13–21; 12:1).

As a general principle, nations carry on their national affairs under the sovereignty of God, and this principle applies even to nations that disregard God in their domestic and foreign policies (Deut. 32:8; Isa. 10:5; 40:15, 28; Jer. 46:28; Dan. 2:21, 37; 4:17, 32, 34–35; 5:21; Acts 17:26; Rom. 9:17, 22–23). Some nations become the objects of God's special care and attention. The Syrians and Philistines as well as the Jews were brought to the lands they inhabited by God himself (Amos 9:7). Edom was punished for treachery towards her kin (Obad.; Ezek. 26:4–5, 12). Egypt's sufferings constituted an interim judgment upon her from the hand of God (Ezek. 26:10; 29:6, 13, 19; 30:4, 10, 19, 26).

The way God treats a nation is often related to the way it reacts to Israel, the chosen nation of God, and to God's acts in its own history. God intervened in the history of such empires as Assyria to effect His will, even using them as His instruments to punish other nations for their sins (Isa. 10:5; 30:31; 37:36; 38:6). God will set aside interim judgment upon a nation if that nation repents, as He did when the people of Nineveh heeded the apocalyptic preaching of Jonah.

Babylonian kings had to learn that God had put them on the throne and thus that they should be humble and grateful rather than self-sufficient and cruel (Dan. 2:21, 37; 4:18, 32, 34–35; 5:12). Even they were used by God as an instrument to punish the Jewish people for their sins. The Babylonians invaded Palestine and forced the two remaining Jewish tribes to go to Babylon. Only this drastic measure "for their good" served finally to wean the Jews away from their idols; they never again worshiped idols after returning from this seventy-year captivity (Jer. 24:5; 25:9–12; 27:5–11; 46:1; 50:11; Dan. 9:1; Hab. 1:1–11). Even after being used as God's instrument in chastising the Jews, Babylon was eventually punished in turn for her sins against God and humanity (Jer. 25:27; Hab. 2).

Biblical writers believed that Persia, which practiced a more humane and tolerant imperial policy than did Babylon, providentially defeated Babylon (Isa. 13:17; 45:1–4), freed the Jews from their captivity, and placed some Jews—Daniel and Nehemiah, for examples—in high government offices. Cyrus was the instrument used by God in returning the Jews to their homeland to rebuild the wall and temple of Jerusalem (Ezra 1:1–3; Isa. 44:28; 45:1). Although human leaders are free to act in history and are morally responsible for their actions, God still can use them to execute His will, even without them being aware of it.

Can it be an accident of history that there was a 400-year interlude between powerful empires in the ancient Near East during which the Jews, under David and Solomon, could build up their own powerful, prosperous state? Before this time the Egyptian empire to the south and the Hittite empire to the North had fought for control of Palestine. After 800 B.C. Assyrian, Babylonian, and Persian empires arose and controlled Palestine.

Battles such as the one at Marathon between the Greeks and the Persians have been pivotal in the development of the cultural heritage that is ours. The battle of Quebec between Louis Joseph de Montcalm and James Wolfe decided that North America would be predominantly Anglo-Saxon and Protestant rather than Latin and Roman Catholic in culture. Saratoga, which brought Spanish and French help to the Thirteen Colonies, made possible the emergence of the United States. The defeat of the Spanish Armada in 1588 allowed England to become a Protestant champion in Europe. The nations that won these battles did so not because they were more moral than their opponents but because in the providence of God they were better fitted to be world leaders.

The Frankish state in the West and the Byzantine Empire in the East succeeded in keeping the Muslims from overrunning Europe and submerging Western culture with Muslim culture. The Turks and the French kept Charles V of Spain so busy during the Reformation that Lutheranism in Germany had the opportunity to survive. England came to surpass Portugal, Spain, France, and Germany in gaining overseas empire. After the American Revolution, England became the first nation voluntarily to grant freedom to the people of her empire. She permitted them to have representative, responsible government and finally granted them independent status, making them free nations voluntarily linked with herself by the symbol of the crown and by cultural similarity. These historical phenomena are not amenable to scientific study, but they are hard to explain apart from a system of historical interpretation that is Christian.

6. Above all, God broke into history in a special way in the incarnation of Christ to give the truth and grace that all men need (John 1:14). Paul wrote that Christ came in "the fulness of the time" (Gal. 4:4; cf. I Tim. 2:6), and other biblical authors used related phrases (Acts 2:22–23; 4:27–28; I Peter 1:20). Christ thus came into history personally, and

the "Word was made flesh." This coming of Christ became a midpoint between creation and consummation in history. The prophets uniformly looked forward to the manifestation of Messiah (Mic. 5:2), and today Christians look back to His first coming and forward to His second (Heb. 9:24, 26, 28). Historians with this perspective reject the classical cyclical view of time, the discontinuity between holy and secular history advocated by the neo-orthodox, and the modern spiral, evolutionary concept propounded by liberal interpreters. The early church believed that Christ's death was an historical event, for it confessed in the Apostles' Creed that Christ had "suffered under Pontius Pilate."

The Gospels of the New Testament are reliable historical records of this intrusion of Christ into history. Such Roman writers as Tacitus, Pliny, Suetonius, and Lucian wittingly or unwittingly testified to the historicity of Christ and to the fact that the Christians looked upon Him as the Son of God. No matter how critical his view of the Bible, an honest historian must admit—as many of the severest critics do—the historicity of most of the Bible records and the important place Christ must be given in any view of history.

The cross of Christ is a *logos* or word of God to man in history (I Cor. 1:18; Mark 10:45). The cross fulfilled the Old Testament sacrifices and provides the ground of human salvation in the present age. By it Christ defeated sin, death, and Satan. The successful invasion of Normandy on D-day made Germany's defeat provisionally sure, but much hard fighting, including the battle of Bastogne, was necessary before its defeat became an actual fact. In like manner Christ is now king in the heart of the Christian, enabling the Christian to defeat Satan in his personal life. But Christ's provisional defeat of evil on the cross will become actual defeat when Christ comes the second time.

The resurrection of Christ constitutes a historical validation of His work (Acts 1:1–2; 10:34–41; 17:2–3; Rom. 1:4; 4:25; I Cor. 15:3–4). After the resurrection Christ appeared to the disciples many times (Acts 1:3; 10:38–41; I Cor. 15:5–8) and even ate with them (Luke 24:36–43; Acts 10:41), and all of these were historical events, according to the Bible. Judas was replaced by Matthias so that there would be the full twelve apostles to witness to the resurrection as a historical event with spiritual significance (Acts 1:22). The early church constantly gave witness to Christ's death and especially His resurrection as objective historical events in time and space (Acts 2:32; 3:14; 4:33; 5:32). Because He was raised from the dead, Christ has all authority in time and history until He comes again to consummate the Christian era (Matt. 11:27–28; 28:18; John 3:33; 13:3). Christ's second coming will be, as was His resurrection, a historical event (I Thess. 4:14).

Modern historians and theologians, such as John W. Montgomery in his *Where Is History Going?* and *The Shape of the Past*[2] and Wolfhart Pannenberg in his many books, argue for an inductive, empirical approach to history because the resurrection is a historical event. Although Pannenberg resembles Jürgen Moltmann in the way he relates faith to history and makes theology futuristic in orientation, Pannenberg emphasizes the resurrection of Christ. Pannenberg thinks that faith is rooted in the past, that the resurrection is historical and is essential to biblical Christianity. There is no discontinuity between secular and salvation history. Christ's resurrection is the key to history. No serious interpreter of history can escape the fact that Christ is a main part of academic as well as what some call holy history. Christ is, in fact, the Lord of history.

7. God's control of history is especially evident in His having chosen a people whose unique task is to confront individuals and nations in history with Christ's claims to their allegiance. The Jews in the Old Testament and the church in the New Testament are the groups chosen by God to fulfill this divine mission.

Nikolai Berdyaev rightly pointed out that the persistence and continuity of the Jewish nation in history is a real problem to the academic historian who ignores revelatory data. This nation, which was chosen by God (Deut. 7:6; Isa. 19:25), originated with Abraham (Gen. 15:13–16). God rescued the Jews from Egypt (Deut. 4:20, 34; 6:12; Amos 9:7) and brought them to Palestine (Deut. 11:12; 20:17–18; Ps. 44:1–3), where during an imperial interlude (1200–800 B.C.) they developed into a powerful nation. Later the Jews were dispersed in God's providence and taken captive "for their good" (Jer. 24:5; cf. 25:9–12; Ezek. 23:9; Dan. 1:2).

2. *Where Is History Going? Essays in Support of the Historical Truth of the Christian Revelation* (Grand Rapids: Zondervan, 1969), pp. 35–36; *The Shape of the Past: An Introduction to Philosophical Historiography* (Ann Arbor, Mich.: Edwards, 1962), pp. 138–39, 236–37.

If Isaiah, Jeremiah, and Ezekiel were alive today, it is likely that they would rejoice over the emergence of the nation Israel in its homeland in 1948 (cf. Isa. 11:11; 27:12; Jer. 31:33, 35–40; Ezek. 37). It may well be that the long period of dispersion and of not having first claim on God's attention (Luke 21:24; Acts 15:14; Rom. 11:25–26) is ending, and that the time is coming when God will more particularly deal with the Jewish nation again. These empirical biblical and historical facts concerning the Jew cannot be ignored by the serious historian.

The historian must also face the fact of the church, the chosen people of the New Testament and a transformed community. The church is more an organism in which Christ dwells in history than an organization. The church was redeemed by the sacrifice of Christ (I Peter 1:18–21) to proclaim God's grace to all men (Matt. 28:18–20; Luke 24:45–48; Acts 1:8; II Cor. 5), to serve in love both fellow Christians and all men (Eph. 2:10; Titus 3:8), to display God's wisdom to the universe (Eph. 3:10), and to glorify God (Eph. 3:20–21). All men are united in the church, a truly international organism that transcends race, skin color, culture, class, rank, and sex (Gal. 3:28; Eph. 2:15, 19, 21–22).

Spiritually and morally transformed people in the church (II Cor. 5:17) were to introduce others to Christ, who could transform them as well. They then were to find proximate solutions to problems, which would lead to a measure of social transformation, and which would become a complete transformation at the coming of Christ. The church was to be the "light" of the world (its social conscience) and "salt" (which would keep the world from dissolving into moral chaos). One must remember that the church converted the barbarians who came into the Roman Empire after A.D. 375. Without the Reformers the Reformation era would have been meaningless. The Puritans transformed religious life in England and New England. Following a revival in the eighteenth century, the English church in the nineteenth century helped reform many social evils and launched and sustained a great century of missionary activity. The church is too often ignored or ridiculed by the historian rather than integrated into the total historical scene as a historical fact.

Because of the seeming compression of time and acceleration of historical events in the modern technological age, even non-Christian historians are talking in apocalyptic terms about the end of history. Historical courses oriented to the future are being offered by an increasing number of educational institutions. Jürgen Moltmann's (1926–) theology of hope, set forth in his book *Theology of Hope,*[3] makes history futuristic but seems to equate revolution rather than Christ's return with the future. Like Oscar Cullman he seems to make eternity simply duration of time. God is becoming rather than One who is. The church must give up the past and become a present and future instrument for reconciling man to man, not man to God. Moltmann has more of Marx than Christ in his system, which calls the church to build Utopia on earth by political action and revolution. But Moltmann does show the manner in which many historians and theologians are striking an apocalyptic, futuristic note.

The Consummation or Solution of History

The revelatory data in the Bible links God and His Son with the solution of history, both at its end and within the course of it in time (I Tim. 6:14–15). Prophecy constituted God's challenge to pagan gods to foretell the future as He did. Biblical history denies, on the one hand, deterministic cyclical recurrences, and, on the other, linear, evolutionary progress through human effort to an earthly Utopia. It instead describes history moving in linear fashion to a cataclysmic, supernatural consummation through divine activity. Christ told the disciples that the Holy Spirit would help them know what to expect in the future (John 16:4, 13; cf. 13:19; 14:29).

This biblical outlook does not ignore change to exalt continuity. It does not exclude the possibility of technological progress through science nor even a limited moral progress in history through the influence of the church as light and salt. It does, however, leave no room for the creation of a perfect society by perfectible man. This noble human dream has never been realized in history and will not be realized except through divine action at the end of history.

Biblical writers find the final solution to the history of the Jewish people, the Gentile nations, and the church in the second coming of Christ. At that time the church will be

3. *Theology of Hope: On the Ground and the Implications of a Christian Eschatology* (New York: Harper and Row, 1967).

taken and will come under judgment; it will not be punished, but the extent of its reward will depend on how well it has carried out its mission in the world (John 14:1–3; I Thess. 4:13–18; I Peter 1:17; cf. I Cor. 3:11–15; II Cor. 5:10; Heb. 9:28). After a time a trouble, the Gentile nations will be judged by Christ because man is accountable to God for his actions (Matt. 25:31–46; John 5:28–29; Acts 17:31; 24:15). Then there will be a period of righteous rule by Christ and His saints, in history and upon the earth, a period marked by the absence of sin (Isa. 11; 65:17; 66:12; Dan. 2:44; Acts 15:13–17; Rev. 11:15; 12:5). Ultimately Christ will, after death and sin have been conquered, return the rule to God the Father, who will finally reign over a universe in which all beings are voluntarily subject to Him as a redeemed, integrated humanity in the eternal kingdom of God (Rom. 11:36; I Cor. 15:24–28; Rev. 11:15; 21:24; 22:3).

The historian cannot afford to ignore all this biblical and historical data as he seeks to impart meaning to his findings. He should study as honestly and objectively as possible the secondary, horizontal factors in history (the economic, human, and geographic) and draw from his data what valid inductions he can. But the ultimate problem of recurrence in history, which was raised by the Greeks and Oswald Spengler, and the problem of change, which was raised by modern optimistic historical thinkers, can only be reconciled in the divine plan of history, which takes into account both secular and religious history without creating the problem of dualism. This will integrate the data of scientific history with the data of revelation and philosophy in a synthesis that gives some ultimate meaning. Facticity in history becomes meaningful in the biblical notion that there is linear, eschatological direction in history instead of cyclical motion or indefinite spirals of progress. God becomes the Creator, Controller, and Consummator of history in His Son Jesus Christ, the Lord of history. The Christian historian, then, not the utopian optimist or the pessimist, is the realist. He is open both to brute historical facts and to revelation.

Annotated Bibliography

The following books, in addition to those by Montgomery already mentioned in this chapter, can be studied profitably.

Donald C. Masters in *The Christian Idea of History* (1962) has a helpful, Christian approach to history. Gordon L. Keyes in *Christian Faith and the Interpretation of History* (1966) displays some insights into the development of a Christian approach to history, but his main interest is the view of Augustine.

PART 3

History as Art

Luke has already been cited as a model for a scientific and philosophic approach to history. He also exemplified the artistic approach. He exhibited a mastery of the Greek language, and he wrote his account "in order." This is more than can be said for some modern historians, whose writings are poorly organized and lacking in stylistic grace. Luke wrote clearly, cogently, coherently, and consistently.

CHAPTER 9

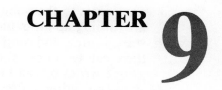

The Historian as Literary Artist

By this time the historian will have carefully researched the records of the incidents he is studying, made some valid inductions from his study of the data, and faced the problem of integrating or interpreting his data in order to create a synthesis that is both meaningful and true to his facts. He now faces the imaginative aspect of his work, imparting in oral or written form both his research and his thought upon it. Writing follows research into and thought about the past. The historian will, as much as is humanly possible, reconstruct the historical past creatively.

The Writing of History

Younger students of history often try to obtain every bit of data about the subject before they begin to write. The writer remembers one person who spent years gathering material for a worthwhile book. Every time he began to write, however, he decided to investigate another facet of his subject, wanting his work to be perfect and complete. When one comes to the point that his reading, study, and thinking are turning up little that is new about his subject, one should start writing and stop worrying about details about which there can be no certainty. Minor details may become clearer as one writes or can be checked before the final rewriting.

The writer's first task is to digest thoroughly, think through, and select from his notes what is directly relevant to his subject. No matter how interesting certain material is to him personally, it should be rigorously excluded if it detracts from the main idea of his work. This is when the modern historian becomes thankful for the elasticity and flexibility of the cards or loose-leaf materials now available for taking notes.

An outline will gradually develop in the writer's mind as he carefully selects his material. The use of a detailed outline will bring clarity and consistency to his thoughts. He should do no writing until he has formulated an outline in his mind and then put it in written form. This outline will be topical, chronological, biographical, or institutional. Notes then can be arranged in the order of the outline, making it even easier to use the material as he writes. His written outline and his reorganized notes will enable the writer to present his material in such a way that the reader will see clearly the woods as well as the individual trees of the writer's thought. This will be particularly true if in his preface or introduction the writer makes his objective clear and even states the basic conclusion or thesis stemming from his research.

He is then ready to begin writing his first or rough draft. More attention should be given in this draft to accuracy of information, correct quotations (which should be short and flow into the text), and corresponding footnotes than to style. The writer should make sure that his facts are properly set forth and are related to his thesis. He can rework this draft later, clearing up details he did not stop to check as he wrote in order to sustain the flow of thought. He can also recheck his materials with his text and add facts that he missed the first time or ideas that come only after a work is completed—even if it is in rough form. With the data corrected on the rough draft, ideas added to it, and the organization clarified on it, this first draft can also serve as the second. This saves the tedium of writing out such a draft. Reworking the rough draft in this manner should lead to completeness.

Grammar, spelling, paragraphing, diction, logic, and coherency will be primary concerns in writing the final draft. A good writer will avoid dangling participles, split infinitives, lack of agreement in the person, number, and case of nouns or pronouns, and improper verb forms. He will also check the spelling of words with care. Proper paragraphing requires that one main idea be stated in a topic sentence, a practice that greatly helps the reader grasp the writer's thought. Paragraphs should be linked to each other with good transitional sentences.

The writer should seek the felicitous phrase and the correct word. He must avoid overusing a pet word, perhaps replacing it with a synonym found in a thesaurus. Words should be chosen because they best express the writer's meaning, not because they display the writer's impressive vocabulary. The great writers, including biblical authors and William Shakespeare, have characteristically used short words rather than long ones. If technical language must be used, its meaning should be made clear.

The text should be written in the third person rather than the first to avoid the excessive use of *I*. The active voice is preferable to the passive, direct sentences to indirect, nouns and verbs to adjectives and adverbs, short sentences to long ones. Antecedents of pronouns should be immediately clear to the reader. The writing style should also be concise. One should never use a paragraph where a sentence will do, a sentence where a phrase will do, or a phrase where a word will do. Verbosity can actually obscure a writer's meaning. A good way to improve one's style is to read the Bible and the works of such historians as Thomas B. Macaulay, George M. Trevelyan, Sir Winston Churchill, and Samuel E. Morison.

Proper emphasis will make the more important points stand out for the reader. These points can be highlighted by discussing them in the preface or introduction, in the conclusion, or at the beginning or end of chapters. The more important an issue, the longer should be the discussion of it. Readers become frustrated with a book or article that is full of details and that fails to assist them in grasping the writer's meaning.

Careful attention given to these matters of grammar and style will result in a work that is clear, compact, concise, and coherent, one that delights as well as informs the reader.

The writer must also make sure that his footnotes follow prescribed style when indicating the source of a fact or idea. Notes also serve to translate a foreign-language sentence in the text, to give the technical definition of a word, to refer the reader to relevant data located elsewhere in the manuscript, to present writers on both sides of a controversial question or obscure matter, to give commentary or supplementary material, and to discuss further a controversial point. Carefully done notes permit the reader or technical scholar to check the author's work or to pursue facets of it that especially interest him.

Appendices can include items of interest or clarification, a discussion of a topic that is too long to be included in the text or the notes, or statistical data. Appendices precede a bibliography.

If a bibliography is included, it should be arranged alphabetically by author under primary and secondary categories, and under these by topics if necessary. Proper style should be followed in each citation. Selected bibliography that includes classified, critical annotations for each source is a joy to the reader who wishes to pursue the subject further.

The final work may take one of several forms, depending on the subject matter and the mode of presentation. Leopold von Ranke popularized the scholarly monograph, a synthesis of reconstruction that deals with a single subject in exhaustive detail and in chronological order. It is based on original or primary documents and is fully documented. Dissertations and learned articles in professional journals are two forms of the monograph.

Texts are secondary syntheses of knowledge for the use of students. Though they are usually written by competent leaders in the field, they often have errors of fact and interpretation.

With vast masses of material becoming available through Ph.D. dissertations and research, cooperative works have become a more prominent form. Under the leadership of a general editor, scholars pool their expertise and each write a chapter in a book or series of books (such as the Cambridge histories), a book in a series (such as The Chronicles of America), or articles in a dictionary or encyclopedia (such as the *International Encyclopedia of the Social Sciences.*)[1]

1. David L. Sills, ed., *International Encyclopedia of the Social Sciences,* 17 vols. (New York: Macmillan, 1968).

Biography and popular narrative history are forms that appeal to many. Biography should relate the subject to his times as well as discuss his life and contribution. Popular history can be written with skill and charm. It is directed to the intelligent layman who reads it either to use it in some way or merely to satisfy his interest and curiosity. Will and Ariel Durant, coauthors of a multivolume history of civilization, have made history live for many people. If the historian wishes his work to count in the marketplace of ideas and the arena of public action, he must try hard to make his work interesting. Only then will people read it and hopefully apply it in becoming better citizens. Historians who write mainly to impress fellow professionals have only themselves to blame when the average man fails to read or pay attention to their work, or when students become so existential in outlook that they see no value in history.

Histories are written in various fields as well as in different forms. Some deal with nations such as England or the United States; some with regions like Latin America or the Middle East; others with such topics as the economic life or diplomatic tradition of a nation; others with periods of time like the ancient or medieval eras; others with civilizations such as Western civilization, Far Eastern civilization, or even world civilization. All of these approaches are helpful, serving the needs of different groups. When reading national or regional histories, one should be especially watchful for the author's national biases or provincialism.

Histories are frequently rewritten and published in revised editions. Ideally these revisions are more extensive than a few additional sentences or paragraphs, corrections, additions to the bibliography, or additions to the last chapter to update the book. Such supposedly new editions are issued simply to make the older editions obsolete and thus to make more money for the author and publisher. There are, however, valid reasons for rewriting. The discovery of new archaeological materials or new documents may require, in the interests of accuracy, that a book be rewritten. The Oxford History of England series (edited by George N. Clark) includes data that was not available to writers of the older Political History of England series (edited by William Hunt and R. L. Poole).

As time passes, men may rise above their personal and environmental biases and be able to review a given subject more objectively. In this way past errors of interpretation may be corrected. Caesar Baronius's and Matthias Flacius's histories of the Reformation are hopelessly partisan when compared with that of Harold J. Grimm.

Minds may be broadened and perspective increased by comparing and contrasting the present with the past. A study of dictators in the Greek states, of those in the Italian city-states of the Renaissance, and of the benevolent, confessional, and dynastic monarch-dictators of eighteenth-century Europe helps one understand better the rash of dictatorships, both leftist and rightist, that have sprung up since World War I in Europe and Asia. Carl Bridenbaugh in *Mitre and Sceptre*[2] threw new light on the American Revolution with his analysis of the role religion played in that revolution, an aspect that had been neglected by historians preoccupied with economic and constitutional issues.

New methods have helped the historian reconstruct the past. Air photography has revealed sites that cannot be seen on the ground. In England this increased historians' understanding of land use in different periods. Computers make possible better content analysis or aid in statistical, demographic, or economic studies. Psychological analysis can help the historian better comprehend the motives of men of the past. New understanding and applications of the laws of evidence followed in the courtroom can be applied to the study of historical evidence. The spade of the archaeologist uncovers new material that periodically forces histories to be rewritten. The historian's methods become more scientific and sophisticated as time goes on. Affluence and the rise of the paperback book have helped build a mass market that also demands more historical materials. For any one of these reasons or for a combination of them, historians have felt impelled to rewrite history.

The Study of History

Intelligent study of history requires that both teacher and student clearly distinguish between fact and interpretation. Some may overstress the factual, but too often mere opinion passes for the latter. Interpretation for the Christian

2. *Mitre and Sceptre: Transatlantic Faiths, Ideas, Personalities, and Politics, 1689–1775* (New York: Oxford University, 1962).

historian and student also requires that the things being studied be finally integrated into a biblical, theistic frame of reference and that their moral implications be explored.

Forms of Instruction

Students should be aware of the different techniques for presenting facts and interpretation. The older, colonial, question-and-answer method of reciting the text gave way to the lecture form of presentation. The lecture is often condemned today, but it remains the most common form in higher education. It can be used to impart knowledge that the text does not, to increase comprehension through good organization, to permit analysis or necessary synthesis of data, and to give the teacher time to evaluate and apply the material. It demands of the teacher an unusual mastery of his field, requiring him to show the student the relationship of the trees to the forest, the parts to the whole. The lecture should supplement, complement, and interpret the data in the text. If the teacher allows the student to interrupt the lecture by raising questions and posing problems, he helps the student learn to think on his feet.

Discussion sections based on the lecture, the text, and any outside reading and work can also be employed. The tutorial involves the student's studying, independently but under a teacher's guidance, a specialized topic of interest to him. In debates, which can bring important issues into focus, students take negative and affirmative positions and the rest of the class and the professor serve as judges. If students have prepared properly, discussion of a specific topic can be a fruitful way to present alternatives and arrive at a conclusion; if they have not, it becomes a mere sharing of ignorance or opinion. The teacher should guide the discussion by asking leading questions and then see that valid conclusions are drawn.

Field trips to museums, historic sites, and libraries help make the student aware of the living quality of history. Visual aids such as maps in two- and three-dimensional forms, film strips, films, slides, time lines, materials projected by an overhead or written on the chalkboard are also valuable teaching aids.

Writing local history (the history of a county, church, or business institution, for examples), which involves the use of questionnaires, the conducting of interviews, and the study of original documents, will attract the more mature and critical student. Some find sociodrama or simulation games useful techniques of instruction.

More advanced students will be exposed to a seminar in which, if it is like the one introduced at the University of Michigan in 1869 by Charles K. Adams, they will study original sources, criticize them, determine what credible information is in them, and then write their conclusions. Their work will then be judged by their peers and the professor.

Students may also be assigned critical book reviews, problem papers, readings in selected sources, term papers, projects, and oral reports. A critical book review is not just a summary of the book's contents, but a statement of the book's thesis and main ideas, its merits, its place in the literature of the field, and its contribution to knowledge. The critique should take into account the author's education and experience as well as his sources, methods, and interpretations. The organization and style of the book must also be considered. Such a review will involve careful, discriminating reading and study.

Term papers deal with a limited topic. They should begin with an introduction, state a thesis, and discuss at length the relevant data and evidence—both primary and secondary. Many of the rules that apply to writing a book also apply to writing a term paper. Understanding these commonly used methods of instruction will help the student get the most out of them.

Reading History

The library is for the student of history what the laboratory is for the student of science. Much of his time is spent simply reading books. By reading he can teach himself, and curiosity and the willingness to study hard rather than daydream will pay intellectual dividends.

The history student must read with understanding. He should first of all give careful attention to how the text or book is organized so that he may become familiar with important dates, locations, persons, events, books cited, ideas, and especially trends or movements of history. Books are often organized along topical lines—how man governs himself and conducts relations with other states, how he makes his living, how he worships (including important religious ideas and institutions), how he relates to others socially in his class and school, how he pursues his intellectual interests in literature and philosophy, and how he expresses artistically his view of himself and his world. These six, all-inclusive areas of human activity can be summarized with the words *politics, economics, religion, society, intellect,* and *art* (the first letters of these words form the acronym *persia,* a convenient mnemonic device). Which of these areas does the book emphasize?

Books may also be arranged chronologically. It must be remembered that periods and dates are devices to aid the memory; people in the past were not aware that they lived in this or that era. The words *ancient, medieval,* and *modern* have been used to describe periods of human existence since they were coined by Christoph Kellner in the seventeenth century. The term *Reformation* describes the religious upheaval between 1517 and 1648 from which Protestantism came. The term *Enlightenment* refers to the era in the eighteenth century when men followed the dictates of reason and believed that man, using science as a tool, can make indefinite progress. These periods often have an objective reality apart from records of them because men have often assumed a particular world and life view in a particular era.

Some eras may be described as natural units. The period from 1789 to 1815 was an era of revolutionary upheaval that affected not only France, where it had its beginnings, but all of Europe. Its consequences troubled Europe significantly until at least 1848.

After discovering and evaluating a book's organization, the student should look for the author's thesis and supporting ideas, his background and education in relation to the book, his assumptions, and his prejudices. One does not read the books of Charles A. Beard long before noting the prominent place he gave to economic motivation in history. A good writer will state his thesis clearly in the preface, introduction, first or last chapter, or even in the table of contents. The student should make sure he comprehends the topic sentences in paragraphs. Finally, thoughtfully criticizing a book is as important as simply grasping its contents; the book may be, rather than true or factual, merely interpretive.

When the student owns the book he is reading, he can make notes in the margin concerning the above points; this will improve the quality of his review. If he has underlined important ideas, he can quickly reread these portions after class and integrate this material with his class notes. Some students prefer to take class notes on the right two-thirds of a page and leave the left third for ideas taken from the text and other sources. In any case, reading should involve understanding rather than mere memorization, although important facts should be given attention.

Taking Notes

Students will take many notes in their academic careers while attending lectures, reading, and doing research. They should early develop a method that will save time and make it easy to use their notes later. Notes may be word-for-word copies, summaries, references, or comments.

Notes may be taken on four- by six-inch cards, on standard sheets cut in half horizontally, or on whole sheets. Sheets that are loose leaf can be used with more elasticity and flexibility. Retyping notes is a waste of time if one has taken them carefully. Only the general themes, the important points in the outline, the evidence, the teacher's interpretation, and bibliography should be recorded. Underlining or starring the points stressed by the lecturer will aid one in reviewing the material before exams. The student should remember the old axiom that reading will make a full mind, speaking a ready person, and writing an exact man. If he sits in class without taking notes, his attention will waver and he will miss what is significant. If he takes good notes and reflects on them after class, his rate of retention will be high.

Study Aids

Maps, especially three-dimensional ones, can help one understand the geographical aspect of history. Such a map reveals, for example, how the North European plain makes both Germany and Russia vulnerable by land. Germany has historically sought the natural boundary of the Rhine in the west. Russia has sought to have a shatter belt of dependent states along her long, western frontier that could absorb an initial invasion and give her time to mobilize. Communist foreign policy differs little on this point from that of the czars of imperial Russia.

Time lines help emphasize important dates and events, persons, or influential books of the past. Charts or diagrams can make concepts clear. The Reformation becomes more understandable when one realizes that it had two manifestations in addition to the familiar one in the state churches of the Anglicans, Reformed (Presbyterians), and Lutherans: one in the free churches of the Anabaptists; the other in the continuing universal Roman Catholic church, which underwent an internal reform and an external reaction to the Protestant movement. These three manifestations can be expressed easily in diagrammatic or chart form. Developments and relationships as well as contrasts and comparisons lend themselves readily to visual form.

Visits to museums and art galleries help make the past live. The author, when teaching ancient history, took several of his classes to the museum of the University of Chicago's Oriental Institute. These trips always stirred a new interest in antiquity, increased students' understanding of it, and revealed its cultural contribution to the present. Travel or study abroad puts the student in living laboratories for historical study, permitting him to view the monuments and relics of the past and to interact with people who still very much reflect their past history and culture.

Taking Examinations

Until some genius develops another technique for motivating a student and finding out what he has gained from his work, the student will face the hurdle of various kinds of examinations. If he has done his work regularly and daily, he will find examinations a challenge rather than an ordeal. He will not panic when they come. He will review the material well during the several days prior to the examination instead of cramming all night before the test and then being too sleepy to do justice to it.

Most subjects can be condensed to one sheet with an organized outline or pattern of significant persons, places, dates, events, books, and ideas. The process of condensation helps fix these things in the mind, making unnecessary the tedious task of pure memorization, which is for naught if the test requires a knowledge of the data in different combinations. Definitions should be thought out for such important, descriptive terms as *scholasticism* and *feudalism*. If students will review together, especially for essay examinations, the cleverer students will learn better by teaching others and the slower students will not be so apt to miss what is really important. The group can often figure out what questions a teacher will ask and draw up ideal answers. Study of any past tests that are available can help the student see what the examiner feels is important and what types of questions he asks.

Examinations usually consist of objective questions, subjective questions, or a combination of these. Objective tests call for recognition and recall. If the student is familiar with the material, he has only to find the correct answer, which is stated in part of the question. Objective tests are made up of items that must be correctly matched; true-false questions (the student might be asked to alter the statements he marks false and make them true); questions in which only one of several items is correct or in which only one is incorrect; or questions in which blanks must be filled in on the basis of clues given in the question. Students should not change their first answer unless they know for certain that it is wrong. In objective examinations, later questions often give clues to the answers to earlier questions.

Subjective or essay examinations demand more writing and a different method of preparation. Here is where group study can be especially helpful. The student should begin taking the test by selecting the question he is best prepared to answer. By the time he finishes with this question, his mind will be warmed up to the task and the remaining answers will come a little easier. Before he begins to write his answer, he should make sure he understands the question, then jot down on scratch paper a brief outline. The outline will keep his mind from wandering and make his answer more intelligible and better organized. He should be careful to answer no more than the question demands and to support all generalizations with appropriate facts. He should try to save enough time to reread and check his answers.

Historical empathy, trying to live oneself into the period, and understanding the material rather than merely memorizing it, make current history as well as examinations more interesting. The student who prepares for examinations in these ways after studying all term will find that examinations are a challenge to his ability and creativity rather than an ordeal inflicted by the teacher.

The Value of History

As the student reaches the end of his academic career, hopefully he will take issue with Georg Hegel's dictum: The only thing that history teaches is that men have never learned anything from history, never acted on principles derived from it. If Hegel were correct, then it would be true that, as George Santayana put it, those who do not remember the past are condemned to repeat it. Augustine considered history valuable to the Christian because it verifies the historical facts on which Christianity is based. Edmund Burke believed that those who do not cherish the memory of their ancestors do not deserve to be remembered by their posterity. Historian Thomas Fuller stated that increasing one's knowledge of history makes it possible to become old in experience without acquiring wrinkles and gray hair or suffering the infirmities of age. These observations are especially pertinent in an era of existentialism, which discounts the past as irrelevant and ignores it.

Nearly all ancient and medieval historians subscribed to the idea that history has a didactic or teaching function for the individual and the group. They thought that the past is prologue to the present. According to Polybius's *Histories,* history will make one a wiser statesman or general; according to Plutarch's *Lives,* a morally better person.[3] Both Livy in *History of Rome* and Tacitus in *Annals* seconded Plutarch's suggestion.[4] Bede believed that reading history will make men act better, and earlier Paul had asserted that history warns us with examples of wrong courses of action (I Cor. 10:6, 11). Paul later told the church at Rome that history is written "for our learning" (Rom. 15:4). Only modern historians who are preoccupied with studying history scientifically to establish facts or who hold relativistic views of history ignore its value in the present.

History links man with his cultural past, which prevents him from being under the sway of the present alone. History may be thought of as travel in time, helping man to understand and appreciate his present culture and institutions and the world scene of which they are a part. He will become aware of the continuity between the present and the past and conscious of the heritage this gives him. It will make him "at home" in the world and free him from a provincialism that might keep him from understanding others. He can better appreciate other people and their cultures. As Arnold J. Toynbee gazed on the ruins of the Parthenon, he sensed the

3. *Histories,* 1:1, 35; 9:2; 12:25; *Lives,* Pericles 2.

4. *Histories,* preface; *Annals,* 3:65.

link between the Greek culture of Pericles and modern civilization. Alexander Pope was partly right when he wrote in his *Essay on Man* (1732–1734) that man should properly study mankind.[5] Not to know what has happened before one was born, said Cicero, condemns one to perpetual childhood. Santayana asserted similarly that he who will not retain experience will forever remain an infant.

One can become a better citizen of both his country and the world as he studies the past. He has a perspective on how the present came to be, and as he plans for the future, he is aware of the many options open to him and society. He can see how dictatorships and inflation in the past have led to disaster and how prudent government has resulted in advance. Vicarious experience is, as Polybius said, cheaper than personal experience, in which wrong choices can result in disaster. Both Harry S. Truman and Sir Winston Churchill, for two examples, profited from their study of the past.

History is, in addition to knowledge of the past, a way of thinking. Historical study can help one develop desirable critical faculties. He will learn how to analyze, weigh, and judge evidence, and how to think in a detached, objective spirit. He will be humble before the immensity of historical knowledge as well as his own ignorance of it. He will be more tolerant and open-minded. Historians are frequently—more often than their numbers in the academic community would warrant—selected for leadership positions in that community. Perhaps their historical studies help give them patience and balance, keeping them open to the new but not devoted to it for its own sake.

Many have found entertainment in reading history that puts them into dialogue with great men of the past. The reader of Francis Parkman's books better appreciates the Anglo-French struggle for North America and life in the forest. Churchill's books dramatically take one through the crises of World Wars I and II.

One will find moral inspiration in the story of David Livingstone dealing with the tribesmen of Central Africa in complete integrity, even when it meant risking his health. The gospel's transformation of individuals like Augustine and of nations like Britain can encourage one who has become overly conscious of the contemporary church's failure and

5. Epistle 2.

weakness. Many events in history suggest that interim judgment makes morality necessary on the national level as well as the individual. Watergate has graphically, one hopes, taught this lesson to the American people as they have watched the tragic fate of leaders from the President to those in lower echelons of government. This may well help one accept a value system based on biblical ethics.

History also has a synthetic function of criticizing and integrating the findings of various social sciences into a broad, historical picture. Newly discovered people of the past (such as the Achaeans), revealed through study and new information, must be located in their proper places in history. Philosophy may develop systems from ideas and theology may seek to comprehend reality with revelatory data, but history integrates the data of time and space. It is a bridge from the past to the present.

Neither should one forget history's vocational and professional uses. Perhaps teaching on various levels is the most obvious example. Another is research, making the past available to the present by studying and synthesizing the remains of the past.

The study of history is an invaluable background for those who intend to enter journalism, the National Park Service, or diplomatic service abroad, or to work in museums, libraries, or archives. It also helps those who are majoring in literature, other social sciences, and linguistic studies to fit their material in an integrated pattern. This is especially true in properly taught courses on the history of civilization, which relate present culture and institutions to their historical antecedents. Ministers have found history a good background for their work and a helpful source of illustrations for their sermons. In general, history is to the group what memory is to the individual. It satisfies one's curiosity about the past, modifies one's conceptions of the present, and influences one's expectations of the future.

Luke has provided a framework that embraces the scientific aspect of history (its materials and methods), the philosophic aspect (the great writers, schools, and philosophies of history), and the artistic aspect (the writing of history for the public). Luke's goal of truth should always be the historian's goal as he attempts to link secondary horizontal data with the vertical ultimates of God and His revelation. Truth is always the historian's aim even though the inadequacy of the data and his own human limitations will prevent him from finding complete truth, from knowing truth comprehensively as God knows it. Accuracy, orderliness, logic, and honesty should be the historian's ideals. He is to study history, as Timothy was to study the Bible, in such a way that he will enjoy not merely the accolades of men but the approval of God. History is the story not only of men acting in time and space but of God working in time to accomplish His will and to benefit man. As Paul wrote, all things are of God, through God, and to God. In Him, change and continuity are linked.

Annotated Bibliography

Geoffrey R. Elton in *The Practice of History* (1967) gave a practical approach to the study, writing, and teaching of history. The second edition of Sherman Kent's *Writing History* (1967) has many helpful ideas in this area. Manuals already mentioned, such as those by Homer C. Hockett and by Jacques Barzun and Henry F. Graff, have much material in this area.

Bibliography

Aydelotte, William O. *Quantification in History*. Reading, Mass.: Addison-Wesley, 1971.

Barnes, Harry E. *A History of Historical Writing*. 2nd ed. New York: Dover, 1963.

Barzun, Jacques, and Graff, Henry F. *The Modern Researcher*. 2nd ed. New York: Harcourt, Brace and World, 1970.

Bassett, John Spencer. *The Middle Group of American Historians*. 1917. Reprint. Freeport, N.Y.: Books for Libraries, 1966.

Bellot, Hugh H. *American History and American Historians: A Review of Recent Contributions to the Interpretation of the History of the United States*. Norman: University of Oklahoma, 1952.

Bernheim, Ernst. *Lehrbuch der historischen Methode: Mit Nachweis der wichtigsten Quellen und Hülfsmittel zum Studium der Geschichte*. Leipzig: Duncker and Humblot, 1889. (Final edition issued in 1908.)

Billias, George A., and Grob, Gerald N., eds. *American History: Retrospect and Prospect.* New York: Free, 1971.

Black, John B. *The Art of History: A Study of Four Great Historians of the Eighteenth Century.* New York: Russell and Russell, 1965.

Bowden, Henry W. *Church History in the Age of Science: Historiographical Patterns in the United States, 1876–1918.* Chapel Hill: University of North Carolina, 1971.

Brooks, Philip C. *Research in Archives: The Use of Unpublished Primary Sources.* Chicago: University of Chicago, 1969.

Bury, John B. *The Ancient Greek Historians.* 1909. Reprint. New York: Dover, 1958.

Cairns, Grace E. *Philosophies of History: Meeting of East and West in Cycle-Pattern Theories of History.* New York: Philosophical, 1962.

Clark, Gordon H. *Historiography, Secular and Religious.* Nutley, N.J.: Craig, 1971.

Conkin, Paul K., and Stromberg, Roland N. *The Heritage and Challenge of History.* New York: Dodd and Mead, 1971.

Donagan, Alan, and Donagan, Barbara, eds. *Philosophy of History.* New York: Macmillan, 1965.

Dray, William H. *Philosophy of History.* Englewood Cliffs, N.J.: Prentice-Hall, 1964.

Elton, Geoffrey R. *The Practice of History.* New York: Crowell, 1967.

Fehl, Noah E. *History and Society.* Hong Kong: Chung Chi College, Chinese University, 1964.

Fitzsimons, Matthew A.; Pundt, Alfred G.; and Nowell, Charles E.: eds. *The Development of Historiography.* Harrisburg, Pa.: Stackpole, 1954.

Foakes-Jackson, Frederick J. *A History of Church History: Studies of Some Historians of the Christian Church.* Cambridge: Heffer, 1939.

François, Michel, et al. *Historical Study in the West: France, Great Britain, Western Germany, the United States.* New York: Appleton-Century-Crofts, 1968.

Gardiner, Patrick, ed. *Theories of History: Readings from Classical and Contemporary Sources.* Glencoe, Ill.: Free, 1959.

Garraghan, Gilbert J. *A Guide to Historical Method.* Edited by Jean Delanglez. New York: Fordham University, 1946.

Gatell, Frank Otto, and Weinstein, Allen, eds. *American Themes: Essays in Historiography.* New York: Oxford University, 1968.

Gee, Wilson. *Social Science Research Methods.* New York: Appleton-Century-Crofts, 1950.

Gooch, George P. *History and Historians in the Nineteenth Century.* 2nd ed. London: Longmans and Green, 1952.

Gottschalk, Louis R. *Understanding History: A Primer of Historical Method.* 2nd ed. New York: Knopf, 1969.

Gottschalk, Louis R.; Kluckhohn, Clyde; and Angell, Robert. *The Use of Personal Documents in History, Anthropology, and Sociology.* New York: Social Science Research Council, 1945.

Grant, Michael. *The Ancient Historians.* New York: Scribner, 1970.

Hale, John R., ed. *The Evolution of British Historiography: From Bacon to Namier.* Cleveland: Meridian, 1964.

Higham, John, ed. *The Reconstruction of American History.* New York: Harper, 1962.

Hockett, Homer C. *The Critical Method in Historical Research and Writing.* New York: Macmillan, 1955.

Holsti, Ole R. *Content Analysis for the Social Sciences and Humanities.* Reading, Mass.: Addison-Wesley, 1969.

Hoselitz, Berthold F., ed. *A Reader's Guide to the Social Sciences.* Glencoe, Ill.: Free, 1959.

Hughes, H. Stuart. *History as Art and as Science: Twin Vistas on the Past.* New York: Harper and Row, 1964.

Hutchinson, William T., ed. *The Marcus W. Jernegan Essays in American Historiography, by His Former Students at the University of Chicago.* Chicago: University of Chicago, 1937.

Kent, Sherman. *Writing History.* 2nd ed. New York: Appleton-Century-Crofts, 1967.

Keyes, Gordon L. *Christian Faith and the Interpretation of History: A Study of St. Augustine's Philosophy of History.* Lincoln: University of Nebraska, 1966.

Kraus, Michael. *The Writing of American History.* Norman: University of Oklahoma, 1953.

Laistner, Max L. W. *The Greater Roman Historians.* Berkeley: University of California, 1947.

Levin, David. *History as Romantic Art: Bancroft, Prescott, Motley, and Parkman.* Stanford, Calif.: Stanford University, 1959.

Löwith, Karl. *Meaning in History: The Theological Implications of the Philosophy of History.* Chicago: University of Chicago, 1949.

Madge, John H. *The Tools of Social Science.* Garden City, N.Y.: Doubleday, 1965.

Marshall, I. Howard. *Luke: Historian and Theologian.* Grand Rapids: Zondervan, 1970.

Marwick, Arthur. *The Nature of History.* New York: Knopf, 1971.

Masters, Donald C. *The Christian Idea of History: A Lecture Delivered Under the Auspices of Waterloo Lutheran University on February 14, 1962.* Waterloo, Ont.: Waterloo Lutheran University, 1962.

Meyerhoff, Hans, ed. *The Philosophy of History in Our Time: An Anthology.* Garden City, N.Y.: Doubleday, 1959.

Milburn, Robert L. P. *Early Christian Interpretations of History.* New York: Harper, 1954.

Montgomery, John W. *The Shape of the Past: An Introduction to Philosophical Historiography.* Ann Arbor, Mich.: Edwards, 1962.

Nash, Ronald H., ed. *Ideas of History.* 2 vols. New York: Dutton, 1969.

Neff, Emery E. *The Poetry of History: The Contribution of Literature and Literary Scholarship to the Writing of History Since Voltaire.* New York: Columbia University, 1947.

Nevins, Allan. *The Gateway to History.* 2nd ed. Chicago: Quadrangle, 1963.

Patrides, C. A. *The Grand Design of God: The Literary Form of the Christian View of History.* Toronto: University of Toronto, 1972.

Robinson, James Harvey. *The New History: Essays Illustrating the Modern Historical Outlook.* New York: Macmillan, 1912.

Rowney, Don Karl, and Graham, James Q., Jr., eds. *Quantitative History: Selected Readings in the Quantitative Analysis of Historical Data.* Homewood, Ill.: Dorsey, 1969.

Salmon, Lucy Maynard. *Historical Material.* Edited by Adelaide Underhill. New York: Oxford University, 1933.

________. *The Newspaper and the Historian.* New York: Oxford University, 1923.

Sanders, Jennings B. *Historical Interpretations and American Historianship.* Yellow Springs, Ohio: Antioch, 1966.

Schmitt, Bernadotte E., ed. *Some Historians of Modern Europe: Essays in Historiography.* 1942. Reprint. Port Washington, N.Y.: Kennikat, 1966.

Senn, Peter R. *Social Science and Its Methods.* Boston: Holbrook, 1971.

Shafer, Robert J., ed. *A Guide to Historical Method.* 2nd ed. Homewood, Ill.: Dorsey, 1974.

Shotwell, James T. *The History of History.* 2nd ed. New York: Columbia University, 1939. (First edition titled *An Introduction to the History of History.*)

Strayer, Joseph R., ed. *The Interpretation of History.* 1943. Reprint. New York: Smith, 1950.

Thompson, James Westfall, and Holm, Bernard J. *A History of Historical Writing.* 2 vols. New York: Macmillan, 1942.

Widgery, Alban G. *Interpretations of History: Confucius to Toynbee.* London: Allen and Unwin, 1961.

Williams, L. F. Rushbrook. *Four Lectures on the Handling of Historical Material.* New York: Longmans and Green, 1917.

Wish, Harvey. *The American Historian: A Social-Intellectual History of the Writing of the American Past.* New York: Oxford University, 1960.

Index of Subjects

Index of Personal Names

DATE DUE

Reserve SPRING 81			
AUG 31 '85			
5/10/86			